SOLOMON'S TEMPLE

THE HOUSE OF THE LORD

LESLIE M. JOHN

SOLOMON'S TEMPLE

THE HOUSE OF THE LORD

LESLIE M. JOHN

My mission is to proclaim the good news of our Lord Jesus Christ as revealed to me through Holy Bible and from various teachers, preachers, and commentators. This is my voluntary service to God in the name of His only begotten Son Lord Jesus Christ.

My mission is to share the knowledge of the Truth of the living God and proclaim the Gospel of Lord Jesus Christ and not converting forcibly anyone to Christianity. One may accept or reject any or part of my writings/teachings. No offense is meant to any individual or any religion or any organization.

This book brings out the marvelous truth about New Testament believer's body, which is God's Temple, wherein Holy Spirit dwells while in the Old Testament Period God descended and dwelt among men in the Tabernacle. David's desire to build a temple for the 'Ark of the Covenant to rest' is fulfilled in Solomon building the magnificent "House of the LORD".

Prophet Isaiah says:

"Thus saith the LORD, The heaven is my throne, and the earth is my footstool: where is the house that ye build unto me? And where is the place of my rest?" (Isaiah 66:1)

Solomon realizes"

"But will God indeed dwell on the earth? Behold, the heaven and heaven of heavens cannot contain thee; how much less this house that I have builded?" (1 Kings 8:27)

Stephen recounts:

"But Solomon built him an house. Howbeit the most High dwelleth not in temples made with hands; as saith the prophet, Heaven is my throne, and earth is my footstool: what house will ye build me? Saith the Lord: or what is the place of my rest?" (Acts 7:47-49)

Scriptures in electronic form are taken from KJV from open domain and from THE HOLY BIBLE, NEW INTERNATIONAL VERSION®, NIV® Copyright © 1973, 1978, 1984, 2011 by Biblica, Inc.® Used by permission. All rights reserved worldwide

ISBN-10: 0989028399

ISBN-13: 978-0-9890283-9-4

Contents

INTRODUCTION

TABERNACLE, SOLOMON'S TEMPLE AND THE CHURCH

It is worth noting the difference between the Tabernacle, Solomon's Temple and the Church before going through the rest of the Chapters.

After Solomon built the temple he said in his prayer of dedication:

"But will God indeed dwell on the earth? Behold, the heaven and heaven of heavens cannot contain thee; how much less this house that I have builded?" (1 Kings 8:27)

It is amazing that the Almighty God who created heaven and who cannot be contained in man-made buildings loved man so much that He sent His only begotten Son for our sake.

God is a Spirit (John 4:24) and He went before the children of Israel by day in a pillar of a cloud and led them; and he went before them in a pillar of fire by night to give them light. (Exodus 13:21).

The LORD went before the children of Israel in a thick cloud in order that the people may hear when He speaks to Moses. (Exodus 19:9)

The LORD dwelt among them unseen by anyone, yet performing miracles and helping them. In the Old Testament period God came and dwelt among the children of Israel and in the New Testament period the incarnate God humbled himself and dwelt among men in the form of man.

"And the LORD descended in the cloud, and stood with him there, and proclaimed the name of the LORD". (Exodus 34:5)

"For the cloud of the LORD was upon the tabernacle by day, and fire was on it by night, in the sight of all the house of Israel, throughout all their journeys". (Exodus 40:38)

"And the Word was made flesh, and dwelt among us, (and we beheld his glory, the glory as of the only begotten of the Father,) full of grace and truth". (John 1:14)

"Who, being in the form of God, thought it not robbery to be equal with God: But made himself of no reputation, and took upon him the form of a servant, and was made in the likeness of men: And being found in fashion as a man, he humbled himself, and became obedient unto death, even the death of the cross". (Philippians 2:6-8)

God, who at sundry times and in divers manners spoke in time past unto the fathers by the prophets, Hath in these last days spoken unto us by his Son, whom he hath appointed heir of all things, by whom also he made the worlds; Who being the brightness of his glory, and the express image of his person, and upholding all things by the word of his power, when he had by himself purged our sins, sat down on the right hand of the Majesty on high; (Hebrews 1:1-3)

THE TABERNACLE

The word 'Tabernacle' means a portable structure, which was also called the 'Sanctuary', where God came and dwelt among Israelites when they journeyed from Egypt to Canaan. God instructed Moses to build this 'Sanctuary' according to His specifications.

God decided the measurements and the elements therein that He may come and dwell therein among His chosen people, the Israelites. The measurements and the details are specified in Exodus25:8-10. According to Hebrews 9:15 Lord Jesus Christ is the mediator of the New Covenant and by means of His death for the redemption of the transgressions of those saints, who believed in "Yahweh", during Old Testament Period, the promise of eternal inheritance for them was assured.

For the New Testament believers also the death of Jesus on the cross of Calvary provided the way for redemption from sin. The sacrifices offered in the Old Testament period were not enough for them to have redemption from their sins, but those sacrifices were the assurances of their future redemption through the blood of Lord Jesus shed for everyone.

A Testament comes into effect after the death of the testator. "For where a testament is, there must also of necessity be the death of the testator". (Hebrews 9:16)

IN THE OUTER COURT

1. Brazen Altar
2. The Laver

IN THE HOLY PLACE

(1) Candlestick (i.e. Seven Stick Lampstand)
(2) The table and the showbread.
(3) The Golden Censer (also called The Golden Altar)

IN THE MOST HOLY PLACE

1. Ark of the Covenant
2. Mercy Seat

ARK OF THE COVENANT

Ark of the Covenant was made of 'shittim wood' overlaid with pure gold inside and outside. It had four rings of gold on the four corners; two rings on one side and other two rings on the other side.

Staves made of shittim wood were put in the rings by the sides of the ark to facilitate the priests to carry it on their shoulders. God told Moses that the Testimony that He gives shall be put in the ark.

MERCY SEAT

The Mercy Seat of pure gold was made and put upon the ark. Two Cherubims of gold were placed on the ark.

One Cherub facing the other and both these Cherubims were placed with their wings stretched covering the Mercy Seat.

The Testimony, which God asked Moses to put inside Ark consisted of:

1. AARON'S ROD THAT BUDDED
2. THE TWO TABLETS UPON WHICH GOD WROTE THE TEN COMMANDMENTS WITH HIS FINGER and,
3. A POT OF MANNA

The details of the measurements of the Ark of the Covenant are mentioned in Exodus Chapter 25. These elements were made the part of the final elements in the temple at Jerusalem.

SOLOMON'S TEMPLE

The size of the Tabernacle was doubled in building the temple by Solomon. The Tabernacle was rectangular in shape with 150 feet in length, 75 feet in breadth and Solomon's Temple was 300 feet in length and 150 feet in breadth. More details are found in 1 Kings Chapter 7

Zachariah prophesied about the future Jerusalem which will be a place of peace for the first time. Instead of nations rising against for war the nations will come and worship the King.

The thousand year rule of King Jesus will be peaceful as was never seen before in the world history. It will be the time when Jews will celebrate the 'feast of the tabernacles' remembering their forefathers who dwelt in booths while they were on their journey from Egypt to Canaan.

God came and dwelt among them. In the millennium Jesus will be the King over united Israel. The House of Israel and the House of Judah will be united and one as was before king Solomon and even better than that inasmuch as there was none other time where such peace exited as it would exit in the millennium under the rule of Jesus Christ.

 "And it shall come to pass, that every one that is left of all the nations which came against Jerusalem shall even go up from year to year to worship the King, the LORD of hosts, and to keep the feast of tabernacles"(Zechariah 14:16)

THE CHURCH

The body of Christ is one and has many members who are the members of that one body, and being many members they are all one body.

The body of Christ is baptized by one Spirit irrespective of whether we are Jews or Gentiles, or bond or free. One part of the body cannot say to the other that it has no need of the other.

Foot cannot call itself separate from the body because it is not hand, nor can eye can call itself separate because it is not ear, nor can any body part say to the other that it has no need of the other part (1 Corinthians 12:12-24).

The whole body suffers if one of its members suffers loss or damage.

Church is not a building or simply a called out people, or congregation, or gathering of citizens, or social gathering, or discussion or debating forum. It is not also the "kingdom of heaven" or "kingdom of God".

The Church is the "Body of Christ". The Church is the "Bride of Christ". Careful observation of Ephesians Chapter 5 gives us the answer that the one who is presenting to Himself is Lord Jesus Christ and He is presenting to Himself a glorious Church that has no spot, or wrinkle of any such thing.

Jesus is expecting from the Church that it should be without blemish.

What is the purpose of Jesus presenting to himself Church without blemish? It is because the Church is His bride, His own possession which was bought with a price and that price was His own blood shed on the cross.

Christ is the head of the Church and He is the savior of the body. The Church is subject unto Jesus Christ, who loved it so much so that he says a husband should love his wife just as He loved the Church. (Ephesians 5:23-25)

Neither in the 'Tabernacle' nor in the 'Solomon's Temple' all the people of Israel could have access to the most holy place. Only the high priest could have access to the most holy place once a year, but the New Testament believer has so greatly privileged that the Almighty God lives in his heart.

CHAPTER 1
THE SACRIFICES OFFERED BY HIGH PRIEST

The LORD said unto Moses to speak to his brother and the LORD gave instructions, to Aaron through Moses, as detailed in the book of Leviticus Chapter 16.

This is the sequence of sacrifices that were to be offered by Aaron, the high priest. The sequence was followed by Jews ever since then until AD 70 when the Temple was destroyed. However, there is not much of evidence that they offer the sacrifices, after AD 70, just as the LORD gave commandment through Moses to Aaron.

During the reign of King Jeroboam, who ruled the Northern Province of Israel and King Rehoboam, who ruled over the Southern Province of Israel after King Solomon, the "House of Israel" was scattered. "The House of Israel" was taken captive by Assyrians, and the "House of Judah" was taken captive by Babylonians.

Later, some who were under the captivity under Babylonians returned to Southern Province of Israel and some preferred to stay in their regions where they were under captivity, perhaps because of the better life they enjoyed there.

Hebrew language was almost extinct and Israel was destroyed beyond recognition. But then, God promised that He will unite "The House of Israel" and "The House of Judah".

Although Israel came back into existence on 14TH May, 1948, yet there is much to happen. There is no evidence that all the children of Israel have come into the land of Israel.

The Jews have very good knowledge about God and the commandments God gave to them through Moses and they are aware of all the ceremonial laws that were described in the Books of Moses.

Yet, it is surprising to note that they neither accept Jesus as their Messiah nor do they offer sacrifices, after AD 70, as detailed in the books of Moses, especially in the book of Leviticus. Because Jesus was born as a Jew and God loved Israelites and called them as His People and the nation as His nation, and also because Bible asks us to pray for the peace of Jerusalem, I also pray for the peace of Jerusalem, I love them and I love Israel.

I wish they all realized that Lord Jesus was divine and fully human when He was on this earth and died for the sake of our sins. He was buried, rose from the dead and ascended into heaven. He is seated on the right hand of the Majesty. He comes back again as soon as all His enemies are brought to His footstool. Scriptures say that if they do not believe Jesus as their Messiah now, they will be brought to their knees to acknowledge Jesus as their Messiah during the period of "Great Tribulation".

Their faith is that on the "Day of Atonement" they remember all their good works done and if the good works done during the past year outweigh their bad works they deem it as their forgiveness of their sins. If they do not sacrifice the offerings just they were asked to do in Leviticus Chapter 16 they owe explanation to the God's word which says:

"Come now, and let us reason together, saith the LORD: though your sins be as scarlet, they shall be as white as snow; though they be red like crimson, they shall be as wool". (Isaiah 1:18)

"But we are all as an unclean thing, and all our righteousnesses are as filthy rags; and we all do fade as a leaf; and our iniquities, like the wind, have taken us away". (Isaiah 64:6)

Here is how they were asked to offer sacrifices as detailed in Leviticus Chapter 16 on the "Day of Atonement".

On the "Day of Atonement" the high priest was to be all alone in the Tabernacle while the congregation waits outside the Tabernacle. There would be no priest to assist him in the sacrifices that he offers on that day. Any one assisting him on this day would be doing it outside the Tabernacle. The offerings are to be made by the high priest with high precision and reverence; otherwise his death was sure instantaneously.

The very fact that their present day high priests are not dying instantaneously for not offering the bullock and a ram for themselves and the Lord's goat as sin offering and confessing upon the live goat the sins of the high priest and the sins of the people followed by its letting loose into the wilderness itself shows that they are in violation of the Mosaic Law.

The high priest starts by washing his flesh in water and putting on linen garments. God commanded to lay aside the beautiful priestly garments of the high priest on this solemn occasion wherein the high priest is seen in a very humble stature, yet performing a very noble and pleasing deed for the Lord, while offering the sacrifices (Leviticus 16:4)

Lord Jesus Christ was stripped and was beaten up to a very humble state, yet performing a very noble and pleasing deed on the cross, while offering his own body and blood for the sake of remission of our sins. God loved us so much so that He gave His only begotten son for this purpose and whoever believes in Him shall not perish but have everlasting life. It is not we who loved Him first but He loved us first.

"And they stripped him, and put on him a scarlet robe". (Matthew 27:28)

The high priest was to take the bullock of the sin offering and make an atonement for him and for his house and kill it as sin offering on the altar (Leviticus 16:6)

Jesus was without any sin and without any blemish born of the Virgin Mary conceived of the Holy Ghost (Matthew 1:20) and, therefore, he did not need any bullock for himself, but He became the Lamb of God and the sacrifice for our sake. John testified of him that He was the Lamb of God who takes away the sin.

The high priest takes a censer full of burning coals of fire from off the altar before the LORD, and his hands full of sweet incense beaten small, and brings it within the veil.

He puts the incense upon the fire before the LORD, so that the cloud of the incense may cover the mercy seat that is upon the ark of the testimony; and if he failed to follow the said method his death was sure.

The blood of the bullock is sprinkled with his finger upon the mercy seat eastward, and he sprinkles the blood before the mercy seat with his finger seven times. He goes back to the altar and kills the goat on which the lot fell as sin offering for the people and takes the blood of the goat within the veil and applies the blood and sprinkles just as he did with the blood of bullock for his own sake (Leviticus 16:15)

Jesus became the propitiation and substitution for our sake and fulfilled two-fold purpose of becoming sacrifice on behalf of us and bearing our sins upon himself as a substitute in our stead.

"Being justified freely by his grace through the redemption that is in Christ Jesus: Whom God hath set forth to be a propitiation through faith in his blood, to declare his righteousness for the remission of sins that are past, through the forbearance of God" (Romans 3:24-25)

It is because the Tabernacle remained in the midst of the children of Israel with all their transgressions and uncleanness, Aaron, the high priest makes atonement for the holy place.

He brings the live goat and lays both his hands upon the head of the live goat, signifying the transference of the sins of himself, and all the people of Israel on to the live goat, and confesses over the live goat all the iniquities of the children of Israel, and all the transgressions and all their sins, and sends it away by the hand of the fit man into the wilderness.

The goat carries the iniquities of all the people of Israel unto a land not inhabited never to return again to the land where the children of Israel lived. The live goat on which the sins are confessed is led outside the camp by a fit man into the wilderness (Leviticus 16:16-19).

He, who lets the goat into the wilderness bathes his flesh in water and afterwards comes into the camp. Notice the shedding of the blood and its sprinkling covered their sins, yet the sins remained in the sanctuary until the high priest transferred the sins onto the live goat which carried the sins far into an uninhabited land.

The letting of the scapegoat into the wilderness is after the high priest changes his garments of linen and puts on his priestly garments and offering of the fat of the sin offering to be burnt upon the altar (Leviticus 16:20-22)

"For he hath made him to be sin for us, who knew no sin; that we might be made the righteousness of God in him". (2 Corinthians 5:21)

After the sin offering is made by the high priest he shall go into the tabernacle of the congregation and changes his clothing. The high priest washes his clothes, and bathes his flesh in water and then he goes into the camp in his priestly garments offers burnt offering.

The high priest then offers burnt offering for himself first and then offers burnt offering for the people and makes atonement for himself and for the people. He burns the fat of the sin offering on the altar and then lets the scapegoat go.

He washes his clothes, bathes his flesh in water and afterward goes into the camp. The rest of the blood of the bullock and the Lord's goat which were killed for making atonement for sin offering will be carried outside the camp.

The skin, their flesh, and their dung shall be burnt in the fire. He who burns the skins their flesh, dung washes his clothes and bathes his flesh in water and then shall come into the camp (Lev 16:27, 28).

This ritual is ordered by God as a statute to be observed on the tenth day of every seventh month in every year. God ordered that the children of Israel should mourn on this day.

This is only one festival where the children of Israel are asked to mourn instead of rejoicing. It is the 'Day of Atonement", which is a national repentance day.

They and the strangers in that land and the sojourners in that land were not supposed to work on this day.

The priest whom the high priest anoints on this day will serve as the High priest next in the stead of his father. He shall make atonement for the holy sanctuary, tabernacle, and the altar, and also priests, and for all the people of the congregation. This ritual was ordered to be a statute to be observed once every year and Aaron did as the LORD gave commandment through Moses.

"But Christ being come an high priest of good things to come, by a greater and more perfect tabernacle, not made with hands, that is to say, not of this building; Neither by the blood of goats and calves, but by his own blood he entered in once into the holy place, having obtained eternal redemption for us". (Hebrews 9:11-12)

For he testifieth, Thou art a priest for ever after the order of Melchisedec. (Hebrews 7:17)

CHAPTER 2
ABRAM MEETS MELCHIZEDEK

Abram was called as "Hebrew" for the first in Genesis Chapter 14 which describes his triumph of the four kings who defeated confederacy of five kings and took Lot and his possessions along with other wealth they looted while dealing with the confederation of five kings.

The reason for this war was that the confederation of five kings rebelled against the four kings who earlier defeated these five kings and made them to serve them.

The four kings of east were: Amraphel, Arioch, Chedorlaomer, and Tidal (Genesis 14:1)

The five kings in Sodom and Gomorrah area were: Bera, Birsha, Shinab, Shemeber, and Bela (Genesis 14:2)

The five kings served the four kings for twelve years and in the thirteenth year they rebelled against those four kings. In the fourteenth year Chedorlaomer one of the four kings along others smote the five kings and took spoils of the land where Lot lived and Lot and others as prisoners. (Genesis 14:5-10)

It was at this time that a person came and told Abram, the Hebrew, about the looting of the wealth of the Sodom and Gomorrah and also of taking captive of his brother's son, Lot and his possessions.

Abram, who lived in Mamre peacefully and Lot, who lived in Sodom and Gomorrah, with his wealth, did not show interest in either party in these wars, but when Lot and his goods were looted Abram decided to wage war against the four kings to deliver his nephew, Lot and his possessions.

Abram had minority of army of trained three hundred and eighteen servants. He boldly went ahead and divided his army into different groups and smote the four kings and their army and pursued them unto Hobah, which is on the left hand of Damascus. He brought back his brother's son Lot and his wealth and also all the goods, and woman and the people.

Abram's victory against those kings was great and it was God who helped him to secure the said victory over the mighty armies of four kings. Several times in the scriptures

it is be seen that numbers on the side of God do not matter when it comes to waging war with mighty men. Gideon' s victory over Midianites, David's victory of Goliath and Philistines, and his victory at Ziklag over Amalekites, the fall of Jericho walls are only few examples to quote.

After the war was over there came two kings to meet Abram after his victory. One was king of Sodom and other was king of Salem. King of Sodom offered Abram wealth and King of Salem offered bread and wine to Abram to have communion with him.

Abram desired to have only the wealth that was stolen by the four kings and rejected rest of the wealth of this world and preferred to have fellowship with king of Salem. This king of Salem was Melchizedek, about whom there is very little description. Melchisedek was king of righteousness and king of peace.

"And Melchizedek king of Salem brought forth bread and wine: and he [was] the priest of the most high God". Genesis 14:18

Surprisingly there appears one whom Scriptures call as "Melchizedek", king of Salem, and he was the priest of the most high God. This priest was even before the Levitical priesthood came into existence. Abram paid tithe of all he got from his victory and Melchizedek blessed him.

There are two views about Melchizedek. One view is that he was Jesus Christ, who appeared to him. Few other times we see Christophany in the Old Testament; that is Lord Jesus Christ appearing in the form of man to help.

One of the three men, who visited Abram was, believed to be Lord Jesus Christ (Genesis 18:1). When Shadrach, Meshach, and Abednego were thrown into fiery furnace King Nebuchadnezzar saw four persons in the fire. The fourth one was believed to be the Lord Jesus Christ protecting the three men. (Daniel 3:22-25).

Another view is that Melchizedek was a man, a type of Jesus Christ, in whom the anti-type Jesus fulfilled the priesthood. There is no mention about the lineage of Melchizedek in scriptures nor is any detailed description of him.

"And Melchizedek king of Salem brought forth bread and wine: and he was the priest of the most high God. And he blessed him, and said, blessed be Abram of the most high God, possessor of heaven and earth: And blessed be the most high God, which hath delivered thine enemies into thy hand. And he gave him tithes of all". (Genesis 14:18-20)

What is interesting here is that Melchizedek brought "bread and wine" to Abram and that reminds us of Lord Jesus Christ who gave to his disciples bread and wine before his crucifixion and said to them "do this in remembrance of me".

"And as they were eating, Jesus took bread, and blessed [it], and brake [it], and gave [it] to the disciples, and said, Take, eat; this is my body. And he took the cup, and gave thanks, and gave [it] to them, saying, Drink ye all of it; for this is my blood of the new testament, which is shed for many for the remission of sins". Matthew 26:26-28

"And he took bread, and gave thanks, and brake [it], and gave unto them, saying, this is my body which is given for you: this do in remembrance of me". Luke 22:19

David prophesied about Jesus and wrote in Psalm 110:4 that Jehovah swore and will not repent of subduing the enemies of Lord Jesus Christ and bringing them to the footstool of Jesus, who was called as a priest for ever after the order of Melchizedek.

"The LORD hath sworn, and will not repent, Thou art a priest for ever after the order of Melchizedek". (Psalms 110:4)

Years later the writer of Hebrews wrote about Melchisedec in Hebrews Chapters 5, 6 and 7.

So also Christ glorified not himself to be made a high priest; but he that said unto him, Thou art my Son, today have I begotten thee. As he saith also in another place, Thou art a priest forever after the order of Melchisedec. (Hebrews 5:5-6)

"Whither the forerunner is for us entered, even Jesus, made a high priest forever after the order of Melchisedec". (Hebrews 6:20)

Aaronic order of priesthood from Levites was not perfect and Jesus became our high priest of the order of Melchisedec and this priesthood is for ever and ever. Lord Jesus Christ is our High Priest and the only mediator between God and men. All the believers in Christ are priest and have access to the most Holy God through Jesus (1 Peter 2:5).

"For he testifieth, Thou art a priest forever after the order of Melchisedec" (Hebrews 7:17)

CHAPTER 3
ROYAL PRIESTHOOD

"But ye are a chosen generation, a royal priesthood, an holy nation, a peculiar people; that ye should shew forth the praises of him who hath called you out of darkness into his marvellous light" (1 Peter 2:9)

1 Peter 2:9 lists the position of believers in the sight of our living God. Believers in Christ are a chosen generation, a royal priesthood, a holy nation, a peculiar people and then it lists the responsibilities of believer towards the One who has given such status before him.

God called us from out of darkness into marvelous light in order that we may worship him, praise him and bear a good testimony for him.

The priests in the Old Testament period were required to offer sacrifices for themselves and then for the congregation which they were heading. It differed as the times changed and the way they offered sacrifices varied in different time periods.

Until the Mosaic Law came into existence individual saints in the Old Testament offered Sacrifices all by themselves that entitled them to be called as priests; and after the Law was proposed the entire congregations of the children of Israel were called the Kingdom of Priests", but because they violated the Law the priestly office was confined to the tribe of Levi.

Aaron and his sons became the priests. The high priest could enter the Most Holy Place in the Tabernacle only once a year on the 'Day of Atonement'.

There are at least four individuals who can be taken for consideration. (1) Noah (2) Abraham (3) Isaac and (4) Jacob

Noah built an altar unto the Lord and offered clean beast, and clean fowl as burnt offerings on the altar. (Genesis 8:20) Abraham took two of his young men with him and Isaac his son and went to offer the burnt offering. (Genesis 22:3).

Isaac built an altar and called upon the name of the Lord, and pitched his tent and his servants digged a well (Genesis 26:25). Jacob offered sacrifice upon the mount and called his brothers to eat bread and they ate the bread. (Genesis 31:54)

Then after the Law was proposed the children of Israel as a whole nation was called "kingdom of priests" (Exodus 19:6) But they violated the Law and antagonized God several times. They worshipped Idols and angered God. Then, God confined priesthood to the Tribe of Levi. Aaron and his sons from the Tribe of Levi were the priests. (Exodus 28:1)

"And hath made us kings and priests unto God and his Father; to him be glory and dominion for ever and ever. Amen". (Revelation 1:6) This shows the priesthood of individual believers in the present age.

The sons of Aaron were anointed. They had on them Ephod, which is a linen apron, bonnet, which is a cap, breastplate, which is a metal piece worn around the body as a defensive armor, and mitre which is a head-band used as a turban.

The stipulations God prescribed for priests were so stringent that they could not violate any of the conditions that God prescribed. These details are mentioned in Exodus Ch. 27, 28 and 29

Lord Jesus Christ was not after the order of Aaron but he was after the order of Melchizedek. While the priesthood of Aaron was limited; the priesthood of Melchizedek is for ever and ever. Even though there are not many references about Melchizedek, yet the references that are found in Genesis 14:18, Psalm 110:4, Hebrews 5:6 and in Hebrews Chapter 7 give us great knowledge about Lord Jesus Christ's Priesthood after the order of Melchizedek. Jesus is Priest, Prophet and King. Jesus became our High Priest because he offered himself as a sacrifice for our sins.

"For every high priest taken from among men is ordained for men in things pertaining to God, that he may offer both gifts and sacrifices for sins" (Hebrews 5:1)

"But into the second went the high priest alone once every year, not without blood, which he offered for himself, and for the errors of the people" (Hebrews 9:7)

"By a new and living way, which he hath consecrated for us, through the veil, that is to say, his flesh" (Hebrews 10:20)

Having therefore, brethren, boldness to enter into the holiest by the blood of Jesus, By a new and living way, which he hath consecrated for us, through the veil, that is to say, his flesh; And having an high priest over the house of God; Let us draw near with a true heart in full assurance of faith, having our hearts sprinkled from an evil conscience, and our bodies washed with pure water. (Hebrews 10:19-22)

According to Levite priesthood a priest could not be king and likewise a King could not be a priest. That is the reason why we see King Saul was not accepted by God as priest.

"And Saul said, Bring hither a burnt offering to me, and peace offerings. And he offered the burnt offering". (1 Samuel 13:9)

The result was seen in 1 Samuel 13:13

"And Samuel said to Saul, Thou hast done foolishly: thou hast not kept the commandment of the LORD thy God, which he commanded thee: for now would the LORD have established thy kingdom upon Israel forever". (1 Samuel 13:13)

Melchizedek king of Salem was not of the order of Levites. Abraham gave him tithe to Melchizedek.

"And Melchizedek king of Salem brought forth bread and wine: and he was the priest of the most high God. And he blessed him, and said, blessed be Abram of the most high God, possessor of heaven and earth: And blessed be the most high God, which hath delivered thine enemies into thy hand. And he gave him tithes of all". (Genesis 14:18-20)

"For this Melchisedec, king of Salem, priest of the most high God, who met Abraham returning from the slaughter of the kings, and blessed him" (Hebrews 7:1)

When Jesus was crucified the veil in the temple was rent into two from top to bottom signifying granting to us access to the Father through the Son of God, who is our High Priest.

There is, therefore, no more a Priest required for us to offer sacrifices on our behalf nor are we required to confess our sins to any Priest in this world in order that he may convey to God our sins to be forgiven.

We are all priests and he has given us the status of "Royal Priesthood" and Lord Jesus Christ is our High Priest and mediator. (Matthew 27:51)

"But Christ being come an high priest of good things to come, by a greater and more perfect tabernacle, not made with hands, that is to say, not of this building" (Hebrews 9:11)

We are given responsibility to offer sacrifices and those sacrifices are presenting our bodies as living sacrifice, holy and acceptable unto God. (Romans 12:1).

We should be ready to help our brethren (1 John 3:16). We should visit the fatherless and widows in their affliction, and keep ourselves without any blemish. (James 1:27). We should offer sacrifices of praises and thanks to God continually. (Hebrews 13:15)

"I exhort therefore, that, first of all, supplications, prayers, intercessions, and giving of thanks, be made for all men". (1 Timothy 2:1)

CHAPTER 4
DAVID'S DESIRE TO BUILD TEMPLE

Cedar wood is incorruptible. Houses made of wooden were considered as posh living Houses in the Old Testament period, more so, if they were made of Cedar wood. King David lived in one such house made of Cedar wood (Ref: 2 Samuel 5:11).

One day David expressed his concern to Nathan the prophet that while he himself was living in a house made of Cedar wood the Ark of God was within the curtains (2 Samuel 7:2).

King David had a desire to build a house for God. The prophet, although he was from God, spoke this time instantaneously without seeking counsel from Him and said to the King that he may do what was in his mind.

However, God spoke to Nathan the prophet and asked him to go and question David, if he was capable of building a house for God to dwell in! Nathan went to David and questioned David if ever God asked the children of Israel to build a house for Him to dwell in the wilderness while the children of Israel journeyed from Egypt to Canaan except that He said to Moses to build a Tabernacle, which was a portable structure, a tent. A portable structure, the tent, which was a Tabernacle, was the place from where God gave instructions to Moses and Aaron.

God asked David to recollect his own position from where he was made to rise. David was a mere shepherd and yet God made him ruler over the children of Israel and not only God was with him but God made his name to be greater than any king upon this earth. All his enemies were cut out of his sight and his name was made great like that of great men who were on the earth.

God said that he will appoint a place for His people Israel and plant them that they would dwell in a place, which they can call their own, and would not allow wicked people to afflict them anymore as they did before. After bringing the children of Israel from out of Egypt into Canaan God commanded judges to be over His people Israel and later after the fall of King Saul David was made the King.

God caused David to rest from all his enemies and sleep along with his fathers peacefully full of age; nonetheless he was 'invalid' and sickly person during his last days.

God promised to build a house for David and as promised He built a dynasty for David and established a covenant with David that his kingdom will be forever.

As David was a man of wars God said that Solomon, David's son, would build a house for the LORD. God also said that if Solomon committed any iniquity he would be chastised with rod of men, and with the stripes of the children of men, but God's mercy will not depart from him.

King David humbled himself after hearing God's word through Nathan the prophet and exalted the name of God by saying:

"Wherefore thou art great, O LORD God: for there is none like thee, neither is there any God beside thee, according to all that we have heard with our ears" (2 Samuel 7:22)

"And let thy name be magnified forever, saying, The LORD of hosts is the God over Israel: and let the house of thy servant David be established before thee" (2 Samuel 7:26)

CHAPTER 5
DAVID'S FERVOR AND ZEAL

"Then David gave to Solomon his son the pattern of the porch, and of the houses thereof, and of the treasuries thereof, and of the upper chambers thereof, and of the inner parlours thereof, and of the place of the mercy seat" (1 Chronicles 28:11)

David's heart for the LORD and his zeal to do service for Him is adorable and our words may fall short of his real desire. He desired to build the temple for the LORD, but God said he cannot do it because his hands, as seen by God, had stains of blood because he was a man of wars.

The LORD was with David and he acknowledged the LORD in all his ways. He failed in certain areas of his life but his zeal for the LORD, worship, service, and dedication to the LORD outweighed his failures. The LORD said that David was a man of His own heart.

Knowing that he cannot build the temple he has done, before his death, what best he could do for the building the House of the LORD. The LORD indeed honored David and attributed the building of the House of the LORD to him even though the physical construction was done by Solomon, his son.

David provided his knowledge, his expertise, his power, and his wealth for the building of the 'House of the LORD'. He gave the pattern and plan and huge amount of wealth that was needed for the building of the temple by his son. He gave by weight for the things that are to be set up.

David admonished Solomon very lovingly yet firmly to be strong and know that God chose him to build a house for the sanctuary and then gave him the pattern of the porch, of house, of the treasuries of God, and the treasuries of the dedicated things, of the upper chambers, of the inner parlors, of the chambers round about, and of the place where mercy seat is to be set. It was not human decision but David gave the plan to Solomon as led by the Spirit.

David said to Solomon that the LORD made him to understand in writing by His hand upon him even the works of the pattern.

David gave Solomon gold by weight for the things of gold, such as those things that are to be in the Holy Holies etc., instruments of all manner of service, silver for all instruments of silver by weight, and for all instruments of every kind of service. He also provided the things that are needed for Levites and Priests, for all the work of service in the House of the LORD, and for all the vessels of service in the House of the LORD. He gave gold by weight for each candlestick of gold and for the lamps of gold and weight of silver for each candlestick of silver and lamp of silver according to their usage. He gave gold by weight for the tables of showbread for every table and likewise silver for the tables of silver.

David also gave pure gold for the flesh-hooks, the bowls, the cups, gold by weight for each basin of gold, and silver by weight for each basin of silver. In addition, David gave refined gold by weight and gold for the pattern of chariot of the cherubims. The cherubims spread their wings towards one another facing opposite to each other covering the ark of the covenant of the LORD.

David advised Solomon once again to be courageous and be strong in the LORD and build the House of the LORD. He said "fear not, nor be dismayed: for the LORD God, even my God, will be with thee; he will not fail thee, nor forsake thee, until thou hast finished all the work for the service of the house of the LORD".

"And David said to Solomon his son, Be strong and of good courage, and do it: fear not, nor be dismayed: for the LORD God, even my God, will be with thee; he will not fail thee, nor forsake thee, until thou hast finished all the work for the service of the house of the LORD" (1 Chronicles 28:20)

CHAPTER 6
THE LORD PERFORMED DAVID'S DESIRE

"And the LORD hath performed his word that he spoke, and I am risen up in the room of David my father, and sit on the throne of Israel, as the LORD promised, and have built an house for the name of the LORD God of Israel" 1 Kings 8:20

After the construction of the temple was complete the Ark of the Covenant was brought into the Holy of Holies of the temple and as soon as the Ark of the Covenant was placed in the Holy of Holies the glory of the LORD filled the HOUSE OF THE LORD.

King Solomon turned his face towards the people and blessed entire congregation of Israel and they all stood in honor of the King. Then, King Solomon spoke saying "Blessed the LORD God of Israel" and continued explaining how God spoke to his father, David, and fulfilled the Promise of choosing David his father to be the ruler over His people Israel.

God did not choose any city of any of the tribes of Israel to build a house for His name to be there in but His purpose was to choose a man, by the name, David, to be the ruler of Israel.

It was not God who asked David to build a house for Him but it was David who purposed in his heart to honor the LORD and build a House for the LORD that the name of the LORD would be there in.

Knowing that David desired to build a house for the LORD, the LORD said to him that it was good that he had a desire to build a house for the LORD but he cannot build it but his son Solomon would build it.

The LORD performed that which was in the heart of David not by David but by his son Solomon. The LORD honored David inasmuch as he had desire to build the house, but because David was a man of wars with his hands full of blood, God said that his son Solomon would build it.

The desire of David was, however, fulfilled and God performed his desire by David's son, Solomon.

It deserves our attention here that God did not desire to build a house for Himself, but David desired that a house be built for the LORD. God honored David's desire but the building was not by David but it was done by David's son, Solomon.

God performed the desire of David and it was attributable to David that he built the house of the LORD although in practice Solomon, David's son built it. Solomon set the..."Ark of the Covenant" in its place. David's throne was established for ever and ever through Solomon.

God spoke to David by the mouth of Nathan the prophet saying...

"And when thy days be fulfilled, and thou shalt sleep with thy fathers, I will set up thy seed after thee, which shall proceed out of thy bowels, and I will establish his kingdom. He shall build a house for my name, and I will stablish the throne of his kingdom forever. I will be his father, and he shall be my son. If he commit iniquity, I will chasten him with the rod of men, and with the stripes of the children of men: But my mercy shall not depart away from him, as I took [it] from Saul, whom I put away before thee. And thine house and thy kingdom shall be established for ever before thee: thy throne shall be established forever. According to all these words, and according to all this vision, so did Nathan speak unto David" 2 Samuel 7:12-17

CHAPTER 7
GOD FORGIVES

David's Psalm116 encourages believers to ponder life in retrospect and the deliverance the LORD wrought upon them from their distress, sin and iniquities.

Not once but several times in his life David was fleeing from his pursuers like Saul and then later in his life from his own son Absalom. In all the occasions when he was fleeing from his persecutors he depended on God for help and his prayers and supplications were answered. God dealt with all his trials and tribulations compassionately and took care of them.

The LORD called David, a man after His own heart. It is so precious to be called by God as a man after His own heart. David was not perfect in his life.

David's adultery with Bathsheba and causing circumstances where in her husband Uriah was killed, had gone on record never to be erased. He numbered his own army once pointing to the fact that his reliance on the LORD diminished. Yet, he was called a man of after God's own heart not because God approved his iniquities, sin and his pride but because David repented of his sin and sought mercy from the LORD.

David says he loved the LORD because He heard his voice and his supplications. The LORD inclined His ear to him and, therefore, he committed to call on the LORD as long as he lived. He recollects that sorrows of death compassed him, and the pains of hell got hold of him. He called upon the name of the LORD to deliver his soul when he was in trouble and sorrow and the LORD delivered him because the LORD was gracious and merciful. David assures, thereafter, that the Lord preserves the humble.

The LORD was good to him when he confessed his sin to Him as we read in Psalm 51

It was when Nathan the prophet went to him and showed him how he has flawed in his walk with God. When the LORD gave him Kingship and the authority to rule over whole of Israel, he fell into his fleshly desire.

David was highly remorseful of his sin and made available his psalm of confession to be sung by the chief musician aloud before the congregation.

David sought God's mercy and prayed to God to blot out his transgressions. He sought multitude of tender mercies and loving kindness from the LORD. David acknowledged his iniquity and prayed for his cleansing. He realized that by yielding to his fleshly desires he sinned against the LORD and done evil.

David also remembered the very condition of every man born on this earth. He says in sin did his mother conceive him and he was shaped in iniquity. This the condition of every human being born on this earth.

Behold, I was shapen in iniquity; and in sin did my mother conceive me. (Psalms 51:5)

Nevertheless, God looks at the heart of a man and searches his thoughts. Man is wicked in his very thoughts and unless he seeks the holy presence of the Lord in his heart he would slowly but surely slide into irretrievable situation of being in sin.

Apostle Paul writes that we all have sinned and fell short of the glory of God. The wages of sin is death but the gift of God is eternal life through Jesus Christ our Lord. There is surely a way to be saved from sin and receive the gift of eternal life.

"That if thou shalt confess with thy mouth the Lord Jesus, and shalt believe in thine heart that God hath raised him from the dead, thou shalt be saved. For with the heart man believeth unto righteousness; and with the mouth confession is made unto salvation" Romans 10:29, 30

CHAPTER 8
THE USURPER REJECTED

Adonijah, had a greater right to the throne than Solomon, yet he was not the one chosen by God. He also attempted to usurp the throne in an unruly and wrong way, which resulted in his dethronement.

Solomon not only spared his life, but gave him possessions. He thus established his throne by mercy. Let us examine ourselves if we are in such situation today!

If we are not chosen by God, we might have to seek the refuge later and seek mercy of those who are chosen by God. Let us remember that the coveted positions are for those, who are chosen by God; not for those who try to usurp. God will cause the usurpers to end in seeking refuge and will send them to retired life. Only those chosen by God will attain the coveted positions and do the will of God.

Here is a story in 1kings 1st chapter. David's first four sons were, Amnon, Chileab, Absalom, and Adonijah. He also had a son through Bathsheba, and that was Solomon.

2nd Samuel chapter 13:28, 29 and chapter 18:24 show the violent deaths Amnon and Absalom suffered. Chileab, must have died in childhood.

Adonijah, the son of David, usurped the throne of David. He began his plotting with the gain of allies; (1) Joab, who David was unable to control, (2) Abiathar the Priest. Adonijah's next scheme was to host feast for his supporters. Vs. 5 reads "...will be king; and prepared him chariots and horsemen to run before him."

David did not know the plotting and the scheming Adonijah was going ahead with. With the help of Abiathar the priest he usurped the kingship. He slew sheep and oxen and fat cattle, called all his brethren the king's sons and all the men of Judah, the king's servants and hosted feast. And he started reigning.

Bathsheba went in unto the king David, did obeisance and told him, about that his throne was usurped by Adonijah. Bathsheba reminded him of his swearing that his son, Solomon, through her, would become the king.

While she was yet talking to her husband, David the king, Nathan the prophet came in. Nathan questioned the king if he had at any time said that Adonijah would become king. He explained to the king how Adonijah, usurped the kingship without sending an invitation to Nathan, the prophet or Zadok, the priest and Benaiah the son of Jehoida, and Solomon.

David rises up then, and says, "Assuredly Solomon thy son shall reign after me, and he shall sit upon my throne in my stead; even so will I certainly do this day".

Bathsheba thanked the king. King David called Zadok the priest, and Nathan the prophet, and Benaiah the son of Jehoida, and in their presence caused Solomon, his son, to sit upon his mule and ride to "Gihon".

Later Zadok, the priest and Nathan the priest anointed Solomon. And, Benaiah the son of Jehoida answered the king, and said, Amen; the LORD God of my lord the king says so too.

As the LORD hath been with my Lord the king, even so be with Solomon, and make his throne greater than the throne of my lord king David. Thus became Solomon the official king over Israel.

⁂

CHAPTER 9
SPEAKING AGAINST GOD'S CHILDREN

At a time when Israelites were receiving good food from Heaven they murmured for meat and God gave them "quails" from the sea so much so that the flesh came out from their teeth before they chewed.

The wrath of the LORD kindled against them and the people suffered great plague. The Lord called the place as "Kibrothhattaavah" because they buried the people who lusted. Then they moved from "Kibrothhattavah to "Hazeroth" where they pitched their tents (Ref. Numbers 11:31-35).

While they were at Hazeroth Miriam, Aaron's sister and Aaron spoke questioned the leadership of Moses and spoke against him because he married an Ethiopian woman. They questioned if God spoke only by Moses and not by them and the LORD heard their complaint.

It was too much to bear for the LORD murmuring against Moses whom He considered as faithful servant in His house. Scripture says Moses was very meek above all the men on the earth.

The LORD was angry with them and ordered Moses, Aaron and Miriam to come out of the Tabernacle. The three came out.

The LORD came down in the pillar of cloud and called Miriam and Aaron and said to them if there was a prophet among them He would speak to him in a dream but Moses was above the name of any prophet and, therefore, the LORD said would speak to him mouth to mouth, not in confusing language and Moses would see the similitude of the LORD while He spoke to him.

The LORD questioned them how that they were not afraid of Moses! The LORD departed from them.

Miriam, who was first to speak against Moses, became leprous, white as snow. Aaron realized the error and prayed to Moses pleading with him not to hold their sin against them. Aaron acknowledging that they have behaved foolishly.

Moses cried to the LORD and pleaded with the LORD to heal her. The greatness, humility in Moses and his intercessory prayer could be very much appreciated here. He was mediated between those who had indignation against him and the LORD.

The LORD was compassionate on Miriam but not before chastising her. She behaved foolishly against God's chosen one and she deserved chastisement as the LORD said.

God questioned Moses if her father had spit on her face, should she not bear shame for seven days and then commanded that Miriam be shut for seven days and then be released to have fellowship with them again.

In compliance to the commandment of God Miriam was shut out of the camp for seven days and then was received into fellowship. After that they moved out from Hazeroth, and pitched in the wilderness of Paran.

The consequences of revolting against God's chosen one were serious. When the LORD who came by the cloud departed Miriam became leper. Aaron acknowledged that the leprosy was the result of their foolishness and sin and prayed for mercy. Moses intervened on behalf of Miriam and Aaron and pleaded with God to heal Miriam. God chastised Miriam by shutting out from the camp for seven days but was received into fellowship thereafter. The people were stuck at Hazeroth for seven more days because of the revolt of Miriam and Aaron. (Ref: Numbers 12:1-16)

CHAPTER 10
THE DEAL

Hiram, king of Tyre was a lover of David (1 kings 5:1).

When Hiram heard that Solomon has become king over all Israel and inherited his father's throne, he sent his servants to Solomon. The King of Israel Solomon made deal with King of Tyre Hiram. By the provisions of the deal Solomon could buy cedar wood from Hiram and in return pay him twenty thousand measures of wheat for food to his household and twenty thousand measures of pure-oil every year until the supplies made available to him.

A measure is called "cor" in Hebrew and it was equivalent to "homer" i.e. ninety gallons.

["Concerning the ordinance of oil, the bath of oil, ye shall offer the tenth part of a bath out of the cor, which is an homer of ten baths; for ten baths are an homer" (Ezekiel 45:14)]

Hiram supplied Cedar wood to David when he built his home. According to the deal between Solomon and Hiram Solomon supplied his servants and slaves to cut the wood and paid for the labor and the cedar wood supplied by Hiram.

Solomon acknowledged that Hiram already knew that David desired to build the temple at Jerusalem for the LORD but could not do so because he was a man of wars and that David waged wars according to the will of the LORD to put all his enemies under his feet.

Solomon said to Hiram that God gave him peace on every side and there was neither adversary nor an enemy or evil on any side. There was very little for Solomon to do except that he had to rule the people of Israel.

As the scriptures Solomon judged troubling litigation with such an ease that it is gone on record for generations to remember. He was wise and had great knowledge. Therefore, in his peaceful days, he purposed to build the temple for the LORD in Jerusalem according to the desire of his father, David.

God said to David that Solomon, whom God would set on the throne in the stead of David, shall build the "House of the LORD".

Solomon, therefore, asked Hiram to command that they hew cedar trees out of Lebanon, while his servants would obey Hiram in achieving the task. Hiram's servants were exceptionally skilled to hew the cedar trees and Lebanon had plenty of cedar trees.

These cedar trees were incorruptible and had medicinal value. David's own house was built with cedar wood and no wonder Solomon desired to have cedar wood for the construction of the House of the LORD.

Solomon and Hiram had a very good relationship with each other and there was great peace. Solomon sent a huge contingency of labor to assist Hiram in cutting the cedar wood and transporting on sea waters from Lebanon to Jaffa, port city at Jerusalem.

In the four hundred and eightieth year after the children of Israel left from Egypt, which was fourth year of Solomon's reign over Israel, in the month of "Zif" which is the second month

Solomon started building the temple and finished its construction in seven years while it took thirteen years to build his own house. (cf. 1 Kings Chapters 5 and 6)

CHAPTER 11
THE GOD OF HEAVENS

There was a man, son of one of the daughters of Dan. His father was from Tyre, and he was skillful in working with gold, silver, brass, iron, stone, timber, and in linen of colors purple, blue, and crimson. He also had great skill in any kind of graving. The man had very good report from Hiram's father, and, therefore, Hiram sent him to King Solomon to work for him to build the temple.

Solomon had a great determination to build the temple for the name of the LORD and Hiram, King of Tyre, who was a great admirer of King David consented to help his son Solomon build the temple.

Solomon's conviction and his determination were of great admiration. He asserted that He will build the house for the name of the LORD, his God, and dedicate it to Him, to burn before Him sweet incense, to place showbread continually before Him, to offer sacrifices to him every morning and every evening, on the Sabbath days, on the New Moon days, on the solemn feasts of the LORD.

Solomon made his desire an ordinance for the people of Israel. He surely said one great fact that the House that he would build for the LORD will be greater than that of all other gods.

Solomon knew very well that the God of heavens, the God of his fathers, cannot be accommodated in a man-made building. He made it known that heaven of heaven cannot contain Him, yet the building would be for only burn sacrifices before the LORD.

The glory of God came down and dwelt with the children of Israel in the "Holy of Holies" of the "Tabernacle" while they were journeying from Egypt to Canaan and the glory of the LORD appeared to Solomon by night and answered his prayers.

The glory of the LORD went before the children of Israel in the form of pillar of cloud by day and pillar of fire by night. The glory of God divided the Red sea into two in order that the children of Israel may walk on the dry land in the midst of the Red Sea and drown Pharaoh and his chariots and army in the waters.

How can the LORD be confined in a house? It is indeed marvelous that the same great God will dwell in the hearts of those who confess their sins to Lord Jesus Christ and accept Him as their savior.

Psalmist says..."The idols of the heathen are silver and gold, the work of men's hands. They have mouths, but they speak not; eyes have they, but they see not; They have ears, but they hear not; neither is there any breath in their mouths. They that make them are like unto them: so is every one that trusteth in them. Bless the LORD, O house of Israel: bless the LORD, O house of Aaron: Bless the LORD, O house of Levi: ye that fear the LORD, bless the LORD. Blessed be the LORD out of Zion, which dwelleth at Jerusalem. Praise ye the LORD" (Psalms 135:15-21)

Hiram gave Solomon Cedar trees, contingency of labor, skillful men, and in return he asked from Solomon that which he had promised. Solomon gave Hiram, as promised, twenty thousand measures of when for food to his household and twenty measures of pure oil every year. There was great peace between Hiram and Solomon and they made a league together. (One measure is one "cor" equivalent to ninety gallons – ref: Ezekiel 45:4)

Solomon raised levy in the form of laborers to work with Hiram and his laborers. The laborers were thirty thousand from the entire population of Israel and he sent ten thousand at a time and they went in turns to be for one moth at work place at Lebanon and two months at home.

Lebanon was known for abundance in cedar wood, which was needed for building the House of the Lord. David's house, the temple, and Solomon's house were built with cedar wood.

In addition, Solomon sent seventy thousand men to bear the burdens, eighty thousand hewers in the mountains and three thousand and three hundred officers to oversee the work while they were with Hiram and his labor. They all worked together and the work was huge. They worked in quarries and sent great stones, expensive stones, and hewed stones to the temple site to lay the foundation of the temple as king commanded. (Ref: 2 Chronicles Ch.2, 1 Kings Chapter 5)

SIGNIFICANCE OF CEDAR IN THE TEMPLE

In the construction of the Temple at Jerusalem, which is also called "House of the Lord" or Solomon's Temple, Cedar Trees were used extensively.

It is interesting to note that Cedar was used in the Old Testament to signify cleansing. The LORD spoke to Moses and commanded that a law given by Him specifically for cleansing the leper shall be followed.

Leprosy signifies sin and the law of the leper as specified by Lord cleanses the leper from his sin when it is followed meticulously. The method is elaborate and cumbersome but it was to be necessarily followed exactly as the LORD commanded.

CHAPTER 12
CAN GOD BE CONFINED TO A TEMPLE

"But will God indeed dwell on the earth? Behold, the heaven and heaven of heavens cannot contain thee; how much less this house that I have builded?" (1 Kings 8:27)

Recounting the worship of idols, and sacrifices of beasts and human bodies to them by the descendants of Patriarchs, whom Stephen refers as 'your fathers', he says that they carried the Tabernacle on their way to the Promised Land, but had developed an idea of confining God to a place and temple.

When Solomon built the temple and some of the elements of the Tabernacle were placed in it, the children of Israel thought that God can be confined to a place.

Stephen was exposing their utter misunderstanding of God when they blamed him that he was speaking against their holy place and the commandments of Moses that allegedly he was trying to break and teaching people to break.

Stephen exposes their folly that they gave their devotion to the host of heaven, and offered sacrifices with delight to the idols. He says that they took up tabernacle of Moloch, a sun-god, and Remphan, a moon or star-god, and worshipped them. He says, that after worshipping such idols they thought the living God can also be confined to a place or to a temple. That was their understanding after Solomon built the temple.

The offering of the worship in the Tabernacle and building of Solomon's temple was in the plan of God, and He wanted the children of Israel to obey and keep his commandments. Yet, the understanding about confining God a place or temple was in error. Stephen, therefore, questions them if it was possible to confine God to a temple built with hands! The LORD said that Heaven was his throne and earth was his footstool and who could make him dwell in a place like Temple.

Thus saith the LORD, The heaven is my throne, and the earth is my footstool: where is the house that ye build unto me? and where is the place of my rest? (Isaiah 66:1)

Heaven is my throne, and earth is my footstool: what house will ye build me? saith the Lord: or what is the place of my rest? (Acts 7:49)

Stephen's point in defense against their false allegations was that they did not have perfect understanding about the temple, and he never said that he would destroy the temple nor did he speak blasphemous words against the holy place or the Law of Moses. Peradventure even if he spoke such words as they alleged him of, he was not in error.

The elders and scribes lodged false allegations against Stephen that he said Jesus of Nazareth would destroy their holy place and change their customs that they derived from Moses. Stephen was innocent, yet he spoke boldly and charged them they were stiff-necked and persecuted their fathers.

CHAPTER 13
YOU SHALL KNOW THE TRUTH

"And ye shall know the truth, and the truth shall make you free". (John 8:32)

The first few verses from John Chapter 8 describe how a woman, who was caught red handedly in the act of prostitution, was brought by Scribes and Pharisees before Jesus, tempting him to determine whether or not she should be punished as per the Law of Moses.

Jesus stooped down and wrote something on the ground as if he did not hear them. (John 8:6) But when they continued asking him he said to them they may cast stones at her to kill her, but only the man who has never committed any sin in his life may cast first stone at her.

None of the accusers threw stones at her and everyone started leaving one by one. Jesus did not condemn the woman and let her go. Scribes and Pharisees still remained there to drag Jesus into debate and catch him on some point and accuse him.

Then Jesus said to Scribes and Pharisees that he was the light of the world and whoever followed him had the light of life and will not walk in darkness. The Pharisees therefore accused him of his birth. When Jesus said to them that He was not alone but he and the Father were one, they did not understand him. They even asked him where his father was.

Jesus told them that the record he bore was true and they knew him not fully well. (John 8:14-15). Jesus was born of the Virgin Mary. Luke 1:35 records... "And the angel answered and said unto her, The Holy Ghost shall come upon thee, and the power of the Highest shall overshadow thee: therefore also that holy thing which shall be born of thee shall be called the Son of God". Jesus is the Son of God.

Jesus said to them that if they knew God they would have known him as well. The argument went on and Pharisees called names and said that he was Samaritan and he had a devil in him. Jesus said that he had no devil in him and they dishonored him but he honored his Father. (John 8:48-50) They did not believe him even though he spoke the Truth.

It can be seen that Jesus was very bold and point blank to give replies to them. Jesus tells them that they need to be freed of their sin.

Scribes and Pharisees boasted in themselves that they are the children of Abraham and they were never under bondage that they should be freed from their sin. They did not remember or were ignorant that their forefathers were in bondage of slavery under Pharaoh in Egypt; they did not remember or were ignorant that they were under the bondage of Assyrians and Babylonians. They were trying to trap Jesus on some point. They were already under the bondage of Roman Government.

Yet, Jesus was making a point that they were under the bondage of sin and they need to be freed of their sin. Scribes and Pharisees did not realize that Jesus was the Messiah and he was the Son of God. They were claiming that God is their Father and Jesus had to tell them bluntly that their father was devil because they could not recognize the Son of God nor could understand his speech. He said their father, who is the devil, was a murderer from the beginning and lived not in the truth because there is no truth in him. (John 8:41-44)

Jesus spoke the truth because He is the Way, He is the Truth and He is the Light. The Pharisees and Scribes lost their patience and were about to harm Jesus. Even as Jesus was speaking these words many believed; yet Scribes and Pharisees went on accusing him and tried to lay hands on him. The time was net yet come, and therefore, no one could do anything to Jesus and he walked away from their midst unharmed.

CHAPTER 14
LORD JESUS SAVES

"And, behold, the veil of the temple was rent in twain from the top to the bottom; and the earth did quake, and the rocks rent" (Matthew 27:51)

It was great love that the God of Heavens and Earth has shown in sending His one and only begotten Son into this world in the form of man and to live among men. It is He who loved me first not that I loved Him, and He chose me before the foundation of the world to be in His fold. This offer of becoming an adopted son is already extended to everyone in the world that whoever accepts Him as Savior will not perish but will have everlasting life.

When we think of the harsh reality of the destiny of those who are not saved and did not accept Lord Jesus Christ as his/her personal Savior by confessing sins to Him we cannot but have concern for them and take the responsibility of proclaiming the Good News of Lord Jesus Christ and share His love and about the Salvation. There is salvation in none other than Lord Jesus Christ alone. (Ref: John 14:6,

"Jesus saith unto him, I am the way, the truth, and the life: no man cometh unto the Father, but by me" (John 14:6, Ephesians 2:4, 1 John 4:10, 1 John 4:19, Matthew 9:29, Matthew 11:5)

Even though Jesus did miracles, yet Jews, who usually took delight in miracles, did not believe on Him as their Messiah, because they thought their Messiah would come like a king in a royal family. Contrary to their expectations Jesus was born as a poor man in the womb of Virgin Mary conceived of the Holy Ghost.

After Jesus grew up and started his ministry at the age of about thirty he chose few and called them to be his disciples. One such disciple was Matthew, who was a Publican; he collected customs and tax. Jews hated tax collectors because they were, in collaboration with authorities, harassing them. But then, this tax collector, Matthew, found grace in the sight of the Lord, and he was called to be one of his disciples.

Matthew willingly accepted the calling from Jesus and instantly responded by following him. At one point of time, when Jesus was sitting with tax collectors and sinners, Pharisees, a learned sect of Jews, questioned him as to why he was sitting with them to eat.

When Jesus heard that question, he answered and said that those who are healthy do not need a physician, but they that are sick need physician. That was to tell them that the righteous do not need Savior, but sinners do need Savior. Basically, Jesus came for his own people, that is, the Jews; but then the salvation is extended to Gentiles also because Jews rejected Jesus as their "Messiah".

The miracles that Jesus would do were prophesied in Isaiah 35:5-6

"Then the eyes of the blind shall be opened, and the ears of the deaf shall be unstopped. Then shall the lame man leap as a hart, and the tongue of the dumb sing: for in the wilderness shall waters break out, and streams in the desert".

The prophecy was fulfilled when Jesus healed the sick. God said to the children of Israel through Moses that if they "hearkened diligently to the LORD", the Lord would not bring upon them any of the diseases that He brought upon Egyptians (Exodus 15:26).

The children of Israel disobeyed God several times and their disobedience needed reconciliation. Adam rebelled against God by transgressing the commandment of God. Bible records that we are all sinners by birth and there is no one righteous.

According to 1 John 1:8

"If we say that we have no sin, we deceive ourselves, and the truth is not in us". The Children of Israel transgressed the commandments of God several times.

CHAPTER 15
WORSHIP THE GOD OF HEAVENS

Thou shalt not bow down thyself to them, nor serve them: for I the LORD thy God am a jealous God, visiting the iniquity of the fathers upon the children unto the third and fourth generation of them that hate me Exodus 20:5

David the king of Israel addressed in his last days all the princes of Israel, the princes of tribes, and the captains of the companies. He called them as his brethren and his people and said to them that he had a desire to build a house of rest for the 'Ark of the covenant of the LORD, and for the footstool of our God.

However, God said to him that he shall not build the house for the name of the LORD because he was a man of war and shed blood. The God of peace, the LORD of hosts desired that a man of peace, Solomon, the son of David build the house for the 'Ark of the covenant' to rest and for the footstool of our God.

The God of heavens, the LORD, who is Jehovah, chose David as king over Israel and, therefore, he as a king over them calls them his brethren and his people and addresses them that he was chosen to be the king over Israel forever. He was chosen from among the brethren born to Jesse his father.

The Lord gave David many sons; however He chose Solomon, his son through Bathsheba to sit upon the throne of the kingdom of the LORD over Israel. David said God chose Solomon to build the 'house of the LORD' and promised that He will be Solomon's Father and Solomon His son. The LORD said He will establish His kingdom forever provided Solomon kept the LORD's commandment and judgments as on that day.

David asks people of Israel in the presence of God, to keep and seek for all the commandments of the LORD in order that they may possess the good land promised to Abraham and leave it as inheritance of their children forever.

The LORD promised as early as in Genesis Chapter 15:18 to Abraham that to his seed God has given the land from the river of Egypt unto the great river, the river Euphrates.

"In the same day the LORD made a covenant with Abram, saying, Unto thy seed have I given this land, from the river of Egypt unto the great river, the river Euphrates" (Genesis 15:18)

Turning to Solomon, his son, David asks him to know the God of his father, the LORD God of Israel, the God of heavens, The God of Abraham, Isaac, and Jacob, and serve Him with perfect heart and with a willing mind. David says to him very firmly that the LORD searches the hearts and understands all the imaginations of the thoughts and if he seeks the LORD he will find Him but if he forsakes He will cast him off forever.

As the history shows Solomon built the temple and his kingdom was glorious in all respects, yet in his last days, he forsook the God of Abraham, Isaac and Jacob, that resulted in very quick deterioration of his kingdom. Solomon's kingdom could not be passed onto his son, Rehoboam just as he took over from his father David. He forsook the living God and lived a worldly life in his later days with his concubines, who encouraged him to worship the idols that which was highly loathsome to the LORD and his kingdom divided into two.

I am the LORD thy God, which have brought thee out of the land of Egypt, out of the house of bondage. Exodus 20:2

And they shall know that I am the LORD their God, that brought them forth out of the land of Egypt, that I may dwell among them: I am the LORD their God. Exodus 29:46

The God of heavens, who is the God of Abraham, Isaac and
Jacob is the Father of our Lord Jesus Christ as the New
Testament says:

That ye may with one mind and one mouth glorify God, even
the Father of our Lord Jesus Christ. Romans 15:6

But to us there is but one God, the Father, of whom are all
things, and we in him; and one Lord Jesus Christ, by whom are
all things, and we by him. 1Corinthians 8:6

Blessed be God, even the Father of our Lord Jesus Christ, the
Father of mercies, and the God of all comfort 2Corinthians 1:3

The God and Father of our Lord Jesus Christ, which is blessed for
evermore, knoweth that I lie not. 2Corinthians 11:31

Lord Jesus Christ is our Mediator and our High Priest.

CHAPTER 16
CLAIM YOUR PROMISES

" Therefore now, LORD God of Israel, keep with thy servant David my father that thou promised him, saying, There shall not fail thee a man in my sight to sit on the throne of Israel; so that thy children take heed to their way, that they walk before me as thou hast walked before me" (1 Kings 8:25)

King Solomon's prayer of dedication of the temple at Jerusalem, which he built in honor of the LORD, is an excellent intercessory prayer as also a wonderful worship.

Although his desire to build the house was a consequence of the desire his father David, he built the temple in perfect peaceful conditions.

While David had to face enemies around and fight with them ever since he took reigns as King and was laid to rest in peaceful conditions, Solomon had perfect peaceful conditions in his time of reign as king over Israel.

Notwithstanding the end days of Solomon were evil he built the temple for honoring the LORD.

Solomon placed the 'Ark of the Covenant' in the 'Holy of Holies' the glory of the LORD filled the Temple and, thereafter he stood before the altar of the LORD, spread forth his hands towards heaven in the presence of the entire congregations of Israel. The very first words he said were an acknowledgement of the greatness of the LORD.

 Solomon said in his prayer of dedication that there is none like the LORD God of Israel either in heaven above, or on the earth beneath. He acknowledged that the LORD keeps covenant and shows mercy towards His servants who walk in His ways in all their sincere worship in truth and spirit. He remembers the covenant God made with his fathers that if they kept the commandments of God He will be with them and bless them.

Earlier in history of Israel Joshua, was seen of commanding the children of Israel to meditate on the word of God every day and follow the LORD. Solomon knew in his heart and proclaimed that the God of Israel keeps promises made with his fathers and he remembered very recent promise God made with his father David and his desire of building the temple will be fulfilled by his son.

David could not build the house but God fulfilled his heart's desire. If only David was not a man of wars, perhaps, he would have built the temple but he was a man of war and that is why God honored David's desire to build the temple which the LORD called "House of the LORD" by David's son, Solomon. Nevertheless, David provided much of infrastructure and financial help to build the temple.

Solomon calls on God to keep the promises He made with David that He will not fail a man who walk before Him in the same way as David did. Solomon did not lose sight of the promises that God made with David his father but claimed those promises for himself and for his people.

God's promises are available for cashing in and use by us in our lives. Let us call upon God and claim the promises that are applicable to us. A bank note is of no use in our wallet unless it is put to use. Similar are the promises lying unclaimed and made to idle. How great are the riches God provided for us but many a time we leave them behind unclaimed. God takes delight in us and wants us to be blessed but there is an action required by us and that is to claim His promises by faith.

CHAPTER 17
GOD BLESSED SOLOMON

Wisdom and knowledge is granted unto thee; and I will give thee riches, and wealth, and honour, such as none of the kings have had that have been before thee, neither shall there any after thee have the like. (2 Chronicles 1:12)

After Solomon became king over all Israel he had a great responsibility of entrusting responsibilities to various officials in his kingdom, and, therefore he spoke to the captains of thousands and of hundreds and to the judges and to every governor in all Israel, the chief of the fathers.

At the time when Solomon took reigns as king over Israel there were two Tabernacles, one at Gibeon, of the pattern of the Tabernacle that God said to Moses to build in the wilderness when they were journeying from Egypt to Canaan that God may come down and dwell with them and protect them, guard them, provide food and shelter for them.

The second tabernacle was in Jerusalem with the original 'ark of the covenant' that David brought from Kirjathjearim and set it in a tent. The people still worshipped at Gibeon and the Temple was yet to be built. The plans to build the temple at Jerusalem were ready but the building did not commence yet.

The brazen altar that was made by Bezaleel, the son of Uri, the son of Hur, was before the Tabernacle of the LORD at Gibeon and, therefore, Solomon and the congregation went to Gibeon to offer burnt offerings. Solomon, by nature was an extravagant man and more so in honoring the LORD in the earlier stages of his life as King. Solomon offered a thousand burnt offerings upon it and the result was that God appeared to him in a dream in the night and said to him as to what should He give to Solomon.

What a great offer by God to Solomon who offered thousand burnt offerings upon the altar to honor God! When God pleases to bestow blessings upon a man who can stop Him doing so?

The God of Heavens is the owner of this universe and everything belongs to Him. Many a time man thinks he could please God by making a conditional promise to offer his wealth in return to the blessings from God, as if God accepts bribe from man. How foolish it is!

Psalmist says:

For thou desirest not sacrifice; else would I give it: thou delightest not in burnt offering. The sacrifices of God are a broken spirit: a broken and a contrite heart, O God, thou wilt not despise. (Psalms 51:16-17)

For every beast of the forest is mine, and the cattle upon a thousand hills. I know all the fowls of the mountains: and the wild beasts of the field are mine. If I were hungry, I would not tell thee: for the world is mine, and the fulness thereof. Will I eat the flesh of bulls, or drink the blood of goats? Offer unto God thanksgiving; and pay thy vows unto the most High: (Psalms 50:10-14)

It is the heart of a man and the intentions of man that sees. He searches the thoughts of man and blesses him accordingly. Lord Jesus considered the poor woman's offering of two mites in the treasury box greater than the pittance of offering from the huge wealth of wealthiest people who offered in the treasury box. (Mark 12:42-43)

Solomon offered to God thousand burnt offerings as thanksgiving out of his love for the LORD and God blessed him.

When God asked Solomon as to what He should give to him, he did not choose riches, or wealth, or honor, nor the life of his enemies or long life, but humbled himself and recognized how God was with his father David, and he asked from the LORD wisdom and knowledge that he may go out and come in before the people of Israel because they were God's people and their number was so great.

God was pleased with Solomon and gave him wisdom and knowledge to rule the people of Israel and in addition, God also gave him riches, wealth and honor.

CHAPTER 18
SOLOMON AND QUEEN SHEBA

"For it came to pass, when Solomon was old, that his wives turned away his heart after other gods: and his heart was not perfect with the LORD his God, as was the heart of David his father. For Solomon went after Ashtoreth the goddess of the Zidonians, and after Milcom the abomination of the Ammonites. And Solomon did evil in the sight of the LORD, and went not fully after the LORD, as did David his father" (1 Kings 11:4-6)

David the son of Jesse reigned over all Israel for forty years, seven years in Hebron, and thirty three years in Jerusalem and had a blessed and peaceful death full of age. He had riches and honor entire his life period and Solomon was made king over all Israel in his stead.

Solomon's heart was right with God when he took over reigns from his father David, who was king over Israel and David made Solomon the king over Israel dethroning the usurper Adonijah.

Adonijah had greater right to become king but he tried to usurp the power against the will of God and David. Adonjah's attempt to rule over Israel failed and David made Solomon the king. The son born to David from Bathsheba out of his lust before marrying her died. Solomon was the legitimate son of David from Bathsheba whom he married.

God strengthened Solomon and magnified him exceedingly. God was with Solomon and Solomon's kingdom prospered to imaginable heights that Queen of Sheba saw him, his wisdom and his kingdom and said she did not hear about him even half of what he was, and how his kingdom was. Queen Sheba admired exceedingly the blessings Solomon had even at the meat at his table, and the close communication he had with his servants, the good treatment he had rendered to the ministers who attended on him, and their apparel, his treatment of cupbearers and their apparel.

Queen Sheba said...

"Blessed be the LORD thy God, which delighted in thee to set thee on his throne, to be king for the LORD thy God: because thy God loved Israel, to establish them forever, therefore made he thee king over them, to do judgment and justice" (2 Chronicles 9:8)

Solomon took over power from his father who was a mighty king blessed abundantly by God. Solomon was equally blessed by God and David. For quite many years of Solomon's life as king he had peace in his kingdom, and blessings from God.

It is very tragic that Solomon's kingdom known for peace and prosperity tumbled down to lowest ebb not because he was not wise enough to rule the kingdom or enemies attacked him, but man's common enemy, the adversary who is Satan, took advantage of weakness of Solomon.

Satan knew the weakness of Solomon and he attacked rightly at that spot that Solomon was not able to withstand the temptations of illegal relationship with many women and following their idols and worshipping them straight against the will of God.

God spoke to Solomon through David that he should worship the God of Abraham, Isaac, and Jacob but Solomon went after other gods later in his life and God forsook him as king.

"And thou, Solomon my son, know thou the God of thy father, and serve him with a perfect heart and with a willing mind: for the LORD searcheth all hearts, and understandeth all the

imaginations of the thoughts: if thou seek him, he will be found
of thee;

CHAPTER 19
SOLOMON'S HUMBLE PRAYER

Solomon's supplications were as follows:

•   The LORD Promised successors to David and his kingdom shall be established forever through Solomon and, therefore, Solomon prays to the LORD to prove it.

•   To open and keep open the 'House of the LORD' day and night, and to hear and answer the prayer that he was about to make looking at the temple ('House of the LORD') at Jerusalem and hear and answer the prayers of the children of Israel and strangers who look toward the temple ('House of the LORD') at Jerusalem and pray.

•   To hear, forgive and answer the prayers of those offenders who sinned against their neighbors and swear an oath at the altar in the temple ('House of the LORD').

•   To hear and answer by 'requiting the wicked by recompensing his way upon his own head and by justifying the righteous by giving him according to his righteousness'.

•   To hear and answer the prayers of the children of Israel when they are put to the worse before the enemy because they sinned against Him when they return and confess the LORD's name and pray and make supplication before the LORD in the temple ('House of the LORD').

•   To hear and answer the prayers of the children of Israel and give them the rain and their inheritance when they make supplication looking toward the temple ('House of the LORD') for rain if the LORD had shut up the heavens from raining because of their sin against the LORD.

- To hear and answer the prayers of the children of Israel when they look toward the temple ('House of the LORD') and pray to take away the dearth in the land, the pestilence, blasting, or mildew, locusts, or caterpillars and if their enemies besiege their cities of their land however sore or whatsoever the sickness there be.

- To hear and answer the prayers of any Israelite who would know his own sore and his grief and spreads his hands seeking mercy in the temple ('House of the LORD').

- To hear and answer the prayers of strangers who are not the children of Israel but come from countries to know the great name and the mighty hand of the LORD when they stretch out their hands to the LORD for mercy in the temple ('House of the LORD').

- To hear and fight for the cause of the children of Israel when they go out for war against their enemies and pray looking toward the temple ('House of the LORD').

- To hear, cease from anger and forgive the sin against God and deliver them from their enemies who may carry them captive unto a far off land or near. (Solomon acknowledges that there is no man who does not sin).

- To hear and answer their prayers when they turn to the LORD and look unto the land that the LORD gave to their fathers, look towards the temple in Jerusalem and ask forgiveness even if they have committed wickedness and were carried away captive.

- To remember the mercies shown to David their father and not turn His face away from them.

CHAPTER 20 SOLOMON'S PRAYER ANSWERED

The acceptance of the sacrifices offered by Solomon was confirmed when fire came down from heaven and consumed the burnt offering and sacrifices. The descent of fire from heaven and consuming the offering indicated God's acceptance of the offering.

On earlier occasions when Moses offered burnt offering, as we read in Leviticus 9:24, fire came down from before the LORD and consumed the offering. Gideon offered burnt offering as we read in Judges 6:21 and the angel of the LORD put forth the end of the staff and touched the flesh. David offered burnt offering on the altar and the LORD accepted his offering by sending fire from heaven onto the altar.

The priests could not enter into the temple when the glory of the LORD filled the house. The children of Israel saw the fire coming down from heaven and consuming the burnt offering and they worshipped God acknowledging God's goodness and by saying that His mercy endures forever.

Solomon offered sacrifice of offering of twenty thousand oxen and hundred thousand and twenty thousand sheep at the time of dedicating the house of the LORD. Here is an important point to note.

The sacrifices that Solomon offered were more in number than the brazen altar could accommodate and, therefore, he sanctified and consecrated the middle of the court that was before the LORD. This kind of huge sacrifice was never offered before when the children of Israel were on their journey in the wilderness for forty years.

Solomon prayed to the LORD hallowing the middle court for offering sacrifices God answered his prayer and accepted the said place i.e. the middle of the court as a place of offering in addition to brazen altar.

The priests waited on their offerings and sounded the trumpets and the Levites played music and all the children of Israel stood before the LORD as a mark of honoring the LORD. Solomon celebrated the feast for seven days and all the children of Israel participated in the festival and were joyous.

The LORD imposed a condition that the children of Israel will necessarily call on the name of the LORD, humble themselves, pray, seek the LORD's face and turn from their wicked ways, then He will hear their prayer and even if he had shut up heaven preventing rain to come down, or if He commanded the locusts to devour the land, or if He sent pestilence among His people He will hear from heaven their supplications and forgive them their sin and will heal their land.

The LORD appeared to Solomon by night and said to him that He heard the prayer and chose the temple at Jerusalem as His place as a "House of Sacrifice" and that His eyes and heart shall be there perpetually.

The LORD said to Solomon very firmly that he should keep the LORD's statues and His judgments in order that the kingdom be established as He has covenanted with David his father by saying that there shall be ever a successor to rule the land of Israel.

However, the LORD said, if he failed to keep the statures and the judgments of the LORD and worship other gods then the LORD will pluck them by the roots out of the land of the LORD will make the land be a proverb and a by word among all nations. The nations will witness that the children of Israel forsook the LORD and worshipped other gods and, therefore, the LORD destroyed their land (Ref: Chronicles 7:12-22)

It is very interesting to note that Daniel opened the windows of his house, looked toward the temple in Jerusalem and prayed for the children of Israel confessing their sins and the LORD heard his prayer and answered his prayer.

"How shall we sing the LORD'S song in a strange land? If I forget thee, O Jerusalem, let my right hand forget [her cunning]. If I do not remember thee, let my tongue cleave to the roof of my mouth" Psalm 137:4-6

But the LORD's answering was conditional and He said If they turned away from the LORD, His commandments and worshipped other gods He would pluck them up by the roots and will cast them out of His sight that they would become a proverb and a byword among nations (Ref. 2 Chronicles 7:19-20)

However, the promise made by God to David remains. The promise was that God will establish Solomon's kingdom forever and the LORD will be his father. If commits iniquity the LORD will chasten with rod of men and stripes of men but His mercy shall not depart away from him.

"He shall build a house for my name, and I will stablish the throne of his kingdom forever. I will be his father, and he shall be my son. If he commit iniquity, I will chasten him with the rod of men, and with the stripes of the children of men: But my mercy shall not depart away from him, as I took it from Saul, whom I put away before thee" (2 Samuel 7:13-15)

Not long after this prayer of Solomon his kingdom declined and fell down beyond recognition because Solomon himself did that which was unpleasant to God. Israel was divided into two kingdoms – the Northern Kingdom ruled by Jeroboam and the

Southern Kingdom ruled by Rehoboam, son of Solomon. Northern Kingdom consisted of the ten tribes and the Southern Kingdom consisted of Judah and Benjamin. Levites merged on both the sides.

Assyrians took captive of the Northern Kingdom and the Babylonians the Southern Kingdom. The House of Israel was scattered and God only knows where they are at present. Later Babylonians defeated Assyrians and the Assyrians were wiped out totally from the face of the earth as the LORD's promise was fulfilled through Prophet Haggai.

Jesus was born in the lineage of the house of David to the Virgin Mary. Nineteen kings of Judah and a Queen of Judah ruled the southern Kingdom and nineteen kings ruled the Northern Kingdom before Lord Jesus, the Son of God came into the world in the form of man as Jewish Messiah but they rejected Him.

After crucifixion of Jesus in AD the temple at Jerusalem was destroyed by Titus and all the sons of Jacob and their descendants were scattered all over the world. In 1948 the Israel became one. However the land promised by God is yet to be regained by them. The LORD made an unconditional covenant with Abraham that He will give to the seed of Abraham the land from the river of Egypt to the great river, the river of Euphrates.

In the same day the LORD made a covenant with Abram, saying, Unto thy seed have I given this land, from the river of Egypt unto the great river, the river Euphrates: (Genesis 15:18)

 For a New Testament believer the hope is through our Lord and Savior Jesus Christ.

"And whatsoever ye shall ask in my name, that will I do, that the Father may be glorified in the Son" (John 14:13)

"But the Comforter, which is the Holy Ghost, whom the Father will send in my name, he shall teach you all things, and bring all things to your remembrance, whatsoever I have said unto you" (John 14:26)

"For the law was given by Moses, but grace and truth came by Jesus Christ. (John 1:17)"

Oh! What a great assurance we have in our Lord Jesus Christ!

"My Father, which gave them me, is greater than all; and no man is able to pluck them out of my Father's hand". (John 10:29)

CHAPTER 21
YOU ARE THE TEMPLE OF GOD

"Know ye not that ye are the temple of God, and that the Spirit of God dwelleth in you?" (1 Corinthians 3:16)

We are the temple of God and Holy Spirit dwells in us. God takes it very serious if His temple is desecrated and dishonored with worldly things. If God's temple is desecrated He will destroy those who have desecrated it.

When God gave woman to Man, the man, Adam said…"… This is now bone of my bones, and flesh of my flesh: she shall be called Woman, because she was taken out of Man. Therefore shall a man leave his father and his mother, and shall cleave unto his wife: and they shall be one flesh". (Genesis 2:23-24)

If a man joins his flesh with another woman, obviously, he is becoming one with her and both have defiles their bodies.

"Know ye not that your bodies are the members of Christ? Shall I then take the members of Christ, and make them the members of a harlot? God forbid. What? Know ye not that he which is joined to a harlot is one body? For two, saith he, shall be one flesh" (1 Corinthians 6:15-16)

Jesus threw away them that sold and bought in the temple. People who came to the temple to worship God used the porch for wrongful purposes and sold merchandise. They did not consider it profane to allow merchandise in the premise of the temple inasmuch as it was easy for them to buy things used for worship and sacrifice, yet on the whole the trade and transactions gave rise to great deal of noise, confusion and disturbance to the true worshippers.

The place was also used by money exchangers to convert Jewish coins in to Roman coins which gave rise to much noise and confusion. This place was also used for selling doves, which are, of course, used as sacrifice elements during worship, yet the scene produced a great deal of noise and confusion.

"And Jesus went into the temple of God, and cast out all them that sold and bought in the temple, and overthrew the tables of the moneychangers, and the seats of them that sold doves, And said unto them, It is written, My house shall be called the house of prayer; but ye have made it a den of thieves" (Matthew 21:12-13)

The merchants misused the porch and the temple area for selling their merchandise thinking that those who need them for worship may use them and this place would be an easy access to them, yet the problem that such merchandise and the transactions within and without the temple area disturbed the worship service, and caused great deal of confusion within the temple.

Much of that devotion that was needed was diverted to the peripherals and a secondary importance was given to worship, whereas it should have received the primary importance. When a diversion from the worship takes place to give importance to peripherals it becomes idolatry.

God does not like His place to be taken by peripherals, no matter how attractive they look like. It was, therefore, Jesus overthrew the tables of money changers, the seats of them that sold doves and cast all of them out of temple.

"If any man defile the temple of God, him shall God destroy; for the temple of God is holy, which temple ye are". (1 Corinthians 3:17)

CHAPTER 22 LEPROSY

METHOD OF CLEANSING

PHASE I – THE CLEANSING

In the day of leper's cleansing he was to be brought to the priest, who would go out of the camp and looks at the plague of the leprosy in the leper.

The priest would then command the leper to bring for himself two birds alive and clean, cedar wood, scarlet and hyssop. At the instructions of the priest the one of the two birds would be killed in an earthen vessel over running water.

The priest would then dip them and the living bird in the blood of the bird that was killed over the running water. He would then sprinkle the blood seven times upon the leper, who was to be cleansed, and pronounce him clean. The priest lets the living bird loose into the open field.

PHASE II – THE WASHING

The leper who was cleansed thus would have to wash his clothes, shave off his hair and wash himself in water; only then the first phase of the cleansing process would be treated as having been completed.

Now in the second phase the leper thus cleansed would go then come into the camp and would wait outside his tent for seven days. On the seventh day he would shave off his head, his beard, his eyebrows, and shave off the hair from his entire body.   The cleansed leper shall, then,   wash his clothes, his body in water and be clean.

PHASE III - PRESENTING BEFORE THE LORD

On the eighth day he takes two he lambs without blemish, one ewe lamb of the first year without blemish and three tenth deals of fine flour for a meat offering, mingled with oil, and one log of oil. It was then the time for the priest to present the one who was cleansed form leprosy before the LORD at the door of the Tabernacle of the congregation.

The priest offers to God sin offering and trespass offering on behalf of the leper to be cleansed. He takes a he lamb, the log of oil and waves them before the LORD and slays it in the place where the sin offering and burnt offering are made.

Some blood of the offering is taken from the trespass offering by the priest who puts it upon the tip of the right ear, right hand and upon the great toe of the leper to be cleansed. The priest then takes the log of oil and pours it on the palm of his left hand and dips his right finger in the oil that is in his left hand and sprinkles it seven times before the LORD.

The rest of the oil which is in the palm of the leper to be cleansed is taken by the priest and puts it upon the right ear, upon the thumb of the right hand and upon the great toe of the right foot of the leper to be cleansed, and the priest makes an atonement for him before the LORD.

The priest then offers sin offering and makes atonement on behalf of the leper to be cleansed and kills burnt offering on his behalf and offers meat offering and burnt offering and shall make atonement for him and thereafter the leper shall be clean. (Ref: Leviticus 14:1-20)

LEPER HEALED

Leprosy is a sign of sin. Notwithstanding any theory the medical science would say about Leprosy it was under the control of God who turn incurable Leprosy as transient that could be arrested and could turn that which could be arrested to last permanently as He wished. Lord Jesus Christ healed leper fully as we read in Matthew 8:2-4.

A leper approached Lord Jesus Christ and worshipped Him and prayed to him that if He willed He can make clean. The leper believed that Lord Jesus Christ can heal him and, therefore, asserted very firmly that if Lord Jesus Christ willed He can heal him. Seeing how the leper believed in Him, Jesus touched him saying, "I will, be thou clean". The man was fully healed of leprosy immediately and was cleansed. Jesus said to him not to tell anyone but go the priest and offer the gift that Moses commanded for a testimony.

1.   The leper worshipped Jesus

2.   The leper prayed to Jesus

3.   The leper acknowledged the Lordship of Jesus

Worship is to bow down and pay respect. The word is translated from Greek transliterated word "proskuneo". (Strong's number 4352), which means to kiss, like a dog licking his master's hand or to prostrate oneself in homage.

It can be seen that the leper prayed to Jesus that if He willed He can make the leper clean. Why did leper use the word 'clean', instead of 'heal'?

Hebrew transliterated word "tahowr" (Hebrew Strong's Number 2889) and Greek transliterated word "katharizo" (Strong's number 2511) mean to cleanse, purge, purify. Obviously leprosy is un-clean, impure, and needs to be purged and cleansed.

There are three things that Jesus told the cleansed leper to do.

1.   Tell No man (Until he sees the priest to show that he was healed of leprosy)

2.   Offer the gift to the priest as Moses commanded

3.   Bear it as a testimony in order that he may be admitted into society (Cf. Lev 14:1-32)

And, behold, there came a leper and worshipped him, saying, Lord, if thou wilt, thou canst make me clean. And Jesus put forth his hand, and touched him, saying, I will; be thou clean. And immediately his leprosy was cleansed. And Jesus saith unto him, See thou tell no man; but go thy way, shew thyself to the priest, and offer the gift that Moses commanded, for a testimony unto them. (Matthew 8:2-4)

CHAPTER 23
VESTURE DIPPED IN BLOOD

"And he saith unto me, Write, Blessed [are] they which are called unto the marriage supper of the Lamb. And he saith unto me, These are the true sayings of God" Revelation 19:9

Vesture dipped in blood" has a reference to Isaiah 63:2 and about the trampling over the enemies of the Lord and the treading the winepress, but before that it is worth considering about the "Lamb".

The Passover Lamb was set aside on the tenth day of the first month of Jewish calendar i.e. the month of "Abib" and was slain on fourteenth day of the month (Ref. Exodus 12:1-6).

The children of Israel applied the blood of the lamb to the lintel posts of the doors of their houses in order that the Lord may Passover that home without killing the first born in the house. The firstborn of the Egyptians including that of Pharaoh was killed by the Lord and then Pharaoh released the children of Israel from the bondage of slavery.

"And it came to pass, that at midnight the LORD smote all the firstborn in the land of Egypt, from the firstborn of Pharaoh that sat on his throne unto the firstborn of the captive that was in the dungeon; and all the firstborn of cattle" (Exodus 12:29)

The typology of the slaying of the Lamb for the redemption of the children of Israel from the bondage of slavery is fulfilled when Lord Jesus Christ was crucified on the cross of Calvary for the redemption of mankind. Whoever believes in Jesus as Savior will have salvation free of cost and whoever rejects Him as savior will perish according to John 3:16

John the Baptist pointed to Lord Jesus Christ and identified Him as the "Lamb of God"

"The next day John seeth Jesus coming unto him, and saith, Behold the Lamb of God, which taketh away the sin of the world" John 1:29

Apostle John saw in his vision as recorded in Revelation Chapter 19:13 that Lord Jesus Christ was clothed with vesture dipped in blood.

"And he [was] clothed with vesture dipped in blood: and his name is called The Word of God"   Revelation 19:13 and His name was "The Word of God".

 "In the beginning was the Word, and the Word was with God, and the Word was God". (John 1:1)

The Word was made flesh and lived among us.

"And the Word was made flesh, and dwelt among us, (and we beheld his glory, the glory as of the only begotten of the Father,) full of grace and truth" (John 1:14)

 Thus we see three important truths about Lord Jesus Christ.

HE IS THE LAMB OF GOD
HIS VESTURE DIPPED IN BLOOD
HIS NAME IS THE WORD OF GOD

Lord Jesus Christ purchased mediatory power by shedding His own blood. He purchased the blood of His enemies over whom He prevailed by shedding His own blood. He defeated Satan at the cross and His name is the Word of God.

God called things into existence and heavens and the earth and all that is therein are created by Him. God created great whales and everything that moves in the waters. Lastly God created man in His own image after His likeness to have dominion over the fish of the sea, over the fowl of the air and over the cattle and over all the earth and every creeping thing that creeps on the earth.

The LORD God did all this by His word and His word brought everything into existence. His word is double-edged sword and by His word He will smite the nations and rule them with a rod of iron. He treads the winepress of fierceness and the wrath of Almighty God.

Lord Jesus Christ will defeat Edomites according to the prophecy in Isaiah 63:1-5 and with dyed garments from Bozrah after trampling and treading on them. He is great and mighty in power in His fury He will trample them in fury and He will have the blood sprinkled on his garments.

It is His day of vengeance upon them. In reply to the question from Prophet Isaiah, the Lord says that He will tread them in His anger trampling them in His fury, and their blood shall be sprinkled upon His garments.

"Wherefore art thou red in thine apparel, and thy garments like him that treadeth in the winefat? I have trodden the winepress alone; and of the people there was none with me: for I will tread them in mine anger, and trample them in my fury; and their blood shall be sprinkled upon my garments, and I will stain all my raiment" (Isaiah 63:2-3)

He is righteous and mighty to save. Bozrah was a chief city in Edom where Edomites, descendants of Esau lived. Bozrah is destroyed and is no more there but the city will rise up in the end days it remains mystery now what the role of this city would be in the days.

Lord Jesus stood before Herod, who was an Edomite, a descendant of Esau, and was mocked at. Herod ridiculed Lord Jesus Christ and sent Him back to Pilate... Pilate excused himself from rendering justice even though he knew that Lord Jesus Christ was innocent and then all the people answered Pilate and said "...His blood be on us, and on our children" (Matthew 27:25).

How could these two mortals escape from being punished for showing injustice to the Lord Jesus Christ? On the day of crucifixion of Lord Jesus Christ Herod and Pilate, who were enemies to each other became friends.

The words of Jews and others inviting the curse of the blood of the Lord Jesus Christ were given unto them as gift when Titus came and destroyed Jerusalem in AD 70 and killed Jews and crucified several of them upside down on the walls of Jerusalem. But, the justice to the Edomites that includes Herod is yet future.

The soldiers of the governor showed divine purpose in stripping Jesus and putting on Him a scarlet robe.

 "And they stripped him, and put on him a scarlet robe" Matthew 27:28

The Blood of Lord Jesus Christ shed on the cross achieved multiple purposes. He defeated Satan at the cross of Calvary. He purchased us with His precious blood and we are saved not with gold or silver but in His blood by grace through faith. He purchased mediatory power and we have access to the Most Holy Place now. He purchased the power to defeat His enemies by shedding His blood on the cross and His name is the Word of God.

The armies, who are the born-again children of God will be clothed in linen, white and clean, and they follow Him from heaven and a sharp sword goes from His mouth and that word will smite the nations. He will rule the nations with rod of iron.

He treads "the winepress and wrath of Almighty God" and His vesture and on His thigh a name will be seen and the name is:

"KING OF KINGS, AND LORD OF LORDS"

(Ref: Revelation 19:13-16)

Tell the story of Redemption to the nations. It is the desire of God.

"And it shall be when thy son asketh thee in time to come, saying, What is this? That thou shalt say unto him, by strength of hand the LORD brought us out from Egypt, from the house of bondage" (Exodus 13:14)

CHAPTER 24
THE CLEANSING

"Jesus saith to him, He that is washed needeth not save to wash [his] feet, but is clean every whit: and ye are clean, but not all" John 13:10

It was the time of the Passover feast when Jesus knew that His hour was come and that He should leave this word to be with the Father. After the supper was over Lord Jesus rose from the supper, laid aside His garments and took a towel and girded Himself.

The Lord poured water into a basin and began to wash the feet of His disciples and to wipe them with the towel that He girded Himself with. The purpose of this basin is the same as that of the "Laver" in the "Tabernacle" and the "Molten Sea" in Solomon's Temple.

Lord Jesus knew that His disciples were given to Him and He loved them unto the end. The devil had entered the heart of Judas Iscariot to betray Lord Jesus, who pointed the fact later that Judas Iscariot was not clean.

When Jesus came to His disciple Simon Peter to wash his feet the disciple wondered if it was not wrong for the Master to wash the feet of the disciple and said that the Master shall not wash his feet. But then, Lord Jesus, the Master, said to Peter that if He did not wash his feet he will have no part with Him.

Simon Peter realized the importance of being washed of his feet by the Lord and said to the Master to wash not only his feet but his hands and head. The Lord said to Peter that he that was already washed fully does not need to be fully washed but cleanse only the feet. There were two reasons seen in this magnanimous act of the Lord. One is that the Master has to humble Himself before the disciples to teach them the lessons of humility. Secondly, the one who was washed fully of his sin does not need to washed again but be cleansed of that area of sin which defiled him.

It is the daily sanctification that a man needs to have. There was another reason seen in this. It was that the Jews took bath before they start celebrating the Passover festival and that they do not need to take bath again before taking part in the feast but cleanse them again.

"So after he had washed their feet, and had taken his garments, and was set down again, he said unto them, Know ye what I have done to you? Ye call me Master and Lord: and ye say well; for [so] I am. If I then, [your] Lord and Master, have washed your feet; ye also ought to wash one another's feet. For I have given you an example, that ye should do as I have done to you" John 13:12-15

The Priest in the Old Testament period cleansed himself after offering sacrifice on the Bronze Altar and before entering into the "Holy Place" and "Most Holy Place" at the "Laver" in the Tabernacle and at the "Molten Sea"

in the Solomon's Temple. Lord Jesus Christ showed to His disciples what humility is like by washing the feet of His disciples before becoming sacrifice on the cross for our sake and thus becoming High Priest for us.

Lord Jesus Christ was without any sin and without any blemish. He was the perfect "Lamb of God", who became sacrifice for our sake and bore our sin upon Himself (Ref. 2 Corinthians 5:21 and Hebrews 4:14-16)

"Seeing then that we have a great high priest, that is passed into the heavens, Jesus the Son of God, let us hold fast our profession. For we have not an high priest which cannot be touched with the feeling of our infirmities; but was in all points tempted like as we are, yet without sin. Let us therefore come boldly unto the throne of grace, that we may obtain mercy, and find grace to help in time of need" (Hebrews 4:14-16)

THE LAVER

Located between the Bronze Altar and the Golden Altar was the 'Laver'. The Bronze Altar was outside the Holy Place while the Golden Altar was inside the 'Holy Place'. The priest had to wash his hands and legs with the water taken out from the laver before entering into the Holy Place to perform the ceremonial rites related to the 'Holy Place' and the 'Most Holy Place'.

The Bronze Altar was the place where the sacrifices were offered and the Golden Altar was the place where incense was offered. The LORD spoke to Moses and said to him that a laver of brass be made and located between the Bronze Altar where the congregation gather and the Golden Altar where incense is offered. The priest may enter the 'Holy Place' only after washing his hands and legs with the water taken out from this laver.

The foot of the 'laver' was to be made of brass and of the looking-glasses of the women, who assembled at the door of the tabernacle.

The looking-glasses of women signified the religious devotion of the woman and the woman participated in this religious tradition with great zeal.

The instructions were that the laver should contain water. Aaron and his sons needed to cleanse their hands and feet at the 'laver' so that they may not die. The washing was necessary before they go near the Golden Altar to minister. They needed to burn the offering made by fire unto the LORD. The instructions from the LORD were so severe that if they did not wash their hands and feet before entering into the 'Holy Place' to burn the offering made by fire unto the LORD they will die, and these instructions were given unto them and to generation to come from his seed. (Ex. 30:17-21; 38:8 and 40:30).

Moses obeyed the LORD and conveyed to the congregation the words of the LORD and then brought Aaron and his sons and washed them with water. (Lev. 8:5-6)

The Psalmist in Psalm 119:9 says, "Wherewithal shall a young man cleanse his way? By taking heed thereto according to thy word".

Christ loved the Church. Apostle Paul exhorts that husbands should love their wives just as Christ loved the Church, which is His bride.

The believers in Christ need to wash themselves before the Lord every day of their sins so that He may sanctify and wash the Assembly (Ekklesia) and present it as glorious entity, pure and holy, without any blemish or wrinkle. (Ephesians 5:25-27).

The necessity of cleansing by the believer in Christ does not give him a license to sin every day and confess of his/her sin as a routine, but the necessity is to live a holy life throughout one's life period, until he/she leaves this world, lest it should mean that the believer is crucifying Jesus every day.

It does not mean that God will not pardon the sins of the believer, who may willfully commit in his/her daily life, but it emphasizes the need to remain holy unto the Lord. If the believer in Christ sins, he/she will certainly lose the rewards in heaven, to the extent that he sinned and as the Lord may decide at His discretion.

The believer is at risk of losing the grace of the Lord, whom he crucifies daily in his/her life. In the Old Testament period whenever there was a trespass of the law he/she died or was put to death under two or three witnesses.

Salvation once gained will never be lost but if any believer renounces the Lord fully and tramples the Son of God, despising the blood of the Lord and his new covenant under which the believer is saved and in addition despise the spirit of grace the consequences are very serious. (Hebrews 10:25-30)

The need for washing from the water of the laver before entering the 'Holy Place' signifies that the dwelling of the LORD in the tabernacle consecrates the place as holy. "In the beginning was the Word, and the Word was with God, and the Word was God. (John 1:1)" and the Word was made flesh and dwelt among us and believer's body is a holy temple for the Lord to dwell.

John testifies that the Word dwelt among us and we beheld His glory, the glory of the only begotten of the Father in heaven. The Word was full of grace and truth. The Word is our Lord, and He is Jesus, our savior.

The children of Israel sang a song unto the LORD, when He delivered from the bondage of slavery under Pharaoh. The song of Moses (Exodus 15:1-10) exalts the name of the LORD, who delivered from them from slavery and triumphant gloriously. He was their strength and song and He became their salvation and their God.

The LORD is the LORD of wars and He had cast Pharaoh's chariots and his host in to the Red Sea. The enemy pursued them but could not prevail. Pharaoh and his army were drowned in the Red Sea. Recounting these facts John in his vision as recorded in Revelation 15:2-3 says that he saw a sea of glass mingled with fire and those, who got victory over the beast and his image and his mark, and over his number of his name, and they stood on the sea of glass, having the harps of God and they sang the song of Moses unto the Lamb of God, saying His works are marvelous and the Lord God Almighty was His name.

Innocent as he was, the most loved disciple of Jesus, Peter did not know the importance of washing of feet by the Lord. Jesus washed the feet of his disciples and taught them as to how to humble oneself and minister to become worthy of the Lord. Peter asked Jesus as to why he was washing their feet and wipe them with the towel, which he used for girding him.

Peter was about to refuse to accept the ministry of Jesus when he attempted to wash his feet, but then Jesus said to him, that if he did not allow Jesus to wash his feet, he had no part with Him. Peter then prayed to Jesus that He may wash not only his feet but also his hands and head. Jesus in turn said to him that he that is already washed needed no full bath but only cleansing. (John 13:5-10).

Every branch that is in Jesus bears fruit and Jesus purges the branch that keeps bearing fruit for him, so that the branch may bring forth more fruit. Jesus cleanses us from our sins every day and makes us worthy to be presented as holy ones before the Majesty in heaven. John 13:5-10 and 15:2-3).

It is the love of God that made Him to send His only begotten Son into this world so that we may be saved. Christ died for us even when we were in sin and were justified by His blood and were saved from the wrath through Him.

We were His enemies, but though Jesus we are reconciled unto the Father in heaven. (Romans 5:8-10).

Therefore, Jesus gave unto the disciples the power to go into the nations and preach the gospel and assured them that He will be with them always. Speaking to the Samaritan woman Jesus said, "But whosoever drinketh of the water that I shall give him shall never thirst; but the water that I shall give him shall be in him a well of water springing up into everlasting life". (John 4:14).

It emphasizes the need to purify our souls and to obey the Word of God, the truth through the Holy Spirit, so that brethren may love one another with pure hearth fervently. (1 Peter 1:22)

(Sub-head 'THE LAVER' is taken from my book "The Tabernacle")

THE MOLTEN SEA

The term "Molten Sea" seems to be confusing. One gets the idea that there is a sea which is melted or something that is liquefied by heat or in a state of fusion but it is not so.

The "Molten Sea" in Solomon's temple is similar to that of "Laver" which was in the Tabernacle. It could be said that the molten sea is an improvised version of 'Laver'.

The main purpose of this molten sea is for priests, who offer sacrifices on the Bronze altar, to take bath and cleanse themselves from the blood stains on their body.

The offering of sacrifices was physical and the animals were killed on the altar. There was great deal of blood-shed when the animals are sacrificed. The "Laver" in the Tabernacle was not as large in size as the molten sea in Solomon's Temple. The molten sea was located on the east side of the Temple outside the porch.

In Exodus Chapter 30:17-21 it is recorded that Aaron and his sons washed their hands and their feet according to the commandment of the LORD conveyed to them through Moses. The metal brass in the Scriptures indicates 'judgment'. The water in the 'Laver' and in the 'Molten Sea' cleansed their hands that offered the sacrifices unto the LORD. The sacrifices were offered in different forms.

It could be any of the five offerings viz. burnt offering, meat offering, peace offering, sin offering, trespass offering. After offering a sacrifice on the altar priest was necessarily to wash his body be cleansed. If he violated cleansing of his body he was put to death by God instantly.

The measurement of Molten Sea, which was circular in shape, was as follows:

Brim to brim: 10 cubits

Height: 5 Cubits

A line of 30 Cubits encompassed it round about.

The molten sea was mounted on twelve oxen, three looking toward north, three looking toward west, three looking toward south, and three looking toward east. The hinder parts of all the oxen were inward. The shape of the molten sea was looked like the work of the brim of a cup

The description of "Molten Sea" is recorded in 2 Chronicles 4:4-6

"It stood upon twelve oxen, three looking toward the north, and three looking toward the west, and three looking toward the south, and three looking toward the east; and the sea was above upon them, and all their hinder parts were inward.

Its thickness was a hand-breadth, and its brim like the work of the brim of a cup, with lily-blossoms; in capacity it held three thousand baths. And he made ten lavers, and put five on the right and five on the left, to wash in them: they rinsed in them what they prepared for the burnt-offering; and the sea was for the priests to wash in" (2 Chronicles 4:4-6)

SANCTIFICATION BY THE WORD

"That he might sanctify and cleanse it with the washing of water by the word" (Ephesians 5:26)

Queen Esther was chosen by King Ahasuerus to be his queen not before she underwent cleansing process for a total period of twelve months; six months with oil of myrrh and six months with sweet odors. It was after queen Vashti banned to appear before the King anymore because she refused to present herself at the feast hosted by the King and to show her beauty before the princes from Persia and Media, the nobles and princes of the provinces and servants who gathered at the feast hosted by him in his third year of reign. King Ahasuerus ruled from India even unto Ethiopia over one hundred seven and twenty provinces. (Ref. Esther 1:1)

When Queen Vashti, who was very beautiful, refused to present herself in the presence of the King and to show her beauty before the dignitaries the king banned her at the behest of Memucan who was one of the seven wise princes of Persia and Media.

King Ahasuerus said that fair young women be sent to him turn by turn to please him and if the king was pleased she would be his queen or else she would be his concubine.

It was a great challenge for Esther to take up the risky task and accepted for cleansing as specified. She successfully passed the test from the King and became his queen. Esther was the daughter of Mordecai's uncle.

Mordecai was a Jew carried away as captive from Jerusalem and they both became very useful instruments in the hands of God to fulfill His desire to redeem the Jews.

This picture was indirectly referred to when Apostle Paul wrote about the Church that needs sanctification with the washing of water by the word. The husband desires that his wife be pure before he married her.

The cleansing of Esther was an allusion to the cleansing of the Church. Paul writes that wives and husbands need to submit one to another in the fear or the Lord; wives to their husbands just as unto the Lord because husband is the head of the wife even as Christ is the head of the Church. Husbands are instructed to love their wives just as Christ also loved the Church and gave Himself for it.

Lord Jesus Christ is the savior and Church is the body and bride of Christ. He is the head of the Church and the Church is His body and each believer is a member of the said body.

Lord Jesus gave His life unto the Church and He keeps sanctifying it and cleansing it with washing of water by the word in order that He may present unto Himself the Church as a glorious bride, without any wrinkle or any spot but as holy and without any blemish.

The sanctification was seen in the Old Testament period when Aaron and his sons washed their hands and their feet. It was the commandment of the LORD who spoke through Moses saying that he should make a "Laver" of brass and make its foot also of brass and fill it with water and place it between the tabernacle of the congregation and the altar.

The high priest and the priests were commanded that when they enter the tabernacle of the congregation they shall wash with water and if they violated God's commandment they died instantly (Ref. Exodus Ch. 30:17-21)

The sanctification is not by the good works of righteousness that we have done but according to His mercy. He saved us and washed us and filed us with the Holy Spirit (Ref. Titus 3:5)

Speaking to His disciples and referring to them as the branches even as it is applicable to us, Lord Jesus Christ said that He is the true vine and the Father is the husbandman.

Every branch that does not bear fruit for Him will be removed from serving Him, but he purges every branch that bears fruit unto Him that it might bring forth more fruit; and then He declares that they are clean through the word that He spoke to them. Jesus warned them that without remaining in Him they can do nothing worth the blessings from Him.

"Now ye are clean through the word which I have spoken unto you" (John 15:3)

"Jesus answered, Verily, verily, I say unto thee, Except a man be born of water and of the Spirit, he cannot enter into the kingdom of God". (John 3:5)

CHAPTER 25
THE TEMPLE AT MOUNT MORIAH

"Then the angel of the LORD commanded Gad to say to David, that David should go up, and set up an altar unto the LORD in the threshing floor of Ornan the Jebusite". (1 Chronicles 21:18)

It is not just a coincidence that Solomon chose the site at Mount Moriah for building the "house for the LORD" but it was according to divine providence.

The LORD appeared David on the Mount Moriah and spoke to him. This was the place which David prepared for an altar for the LORD on the threshing-floor of Ornan, the jebusite. There is an interesting reason why this site was chosen.

David bought the site at a full price from Ornan, the Jebusite and built an altar for the LORD and offered burnt offering for the offense he committed by numbering his army. David said to Ornan that he desired to have his threshing floor. Ornan offered it free of cost, but, nay David did not accept it for free. David paid full price for the place.

"And Ornan said unto David, Take it to thee, and let my lord the king do that which is good in his eyes: lo, I give thee the oxen also for burnt offerings, and the threshing instruments for wood, and the wheat for the meat offering; I give it all. And King David said to Ornan, Nay; but I will verily buy it for the full price: for I will not take that which is thine for the LORD, nor offer burnt offerings without cost". (1 Chronicles 21:23-24)

Abraham took his son, Isaac, at the commandment of the LORD to sacrifice him as burnt offering to the LORD and as Isaac went along with his father he asked his father that they have fire, the wood but where was the lamb for a burnt offering. Abraham replied Isaac saying God will provide for Himself a lamb for burnt offering. (Ref. Genesis 22:7-8)

Many years later the Father in heaven provided for Himself His own Son, Lord Jesus Christ, as the 'Lamb of God' as sacrifice to bear our sin upon Him. Just as the Lamb was slain as burnt offering by Abraham at Mount Moriah on the Altar, and he called the place as "jehovahjireh", much later Solomon offering huge burnt offering on the Brazen altar at the temple, while inaugurating it after construction, acknowledged the temple as the 'House of the LORD'.

Mount Moriah and Mount Calvary are of much familiar names as our Lord Jesus Christ was crucified on the Golgotha, a place of skull, outside the city, which the Gospel writer Luke called it as 'Calvary'.

Jesus was crucified at a place where criminals were crucified. (References: Chief baker's execution is detailed in Genesis 40:22, Jezebel's execution is detailed in 2 Kings 9:35 and Lord Jesus Christ's crucifixion along with two malefactors was detailed Luke 23:23)

THE GRANDEUR OF THE TEMPLE

Solomon began building the temple on the second day of the second month, in the fourth year of his reign. It was 480th year after the children of Israel had come out of the land of Egypt. The measurements of the temple were as follows:

Length by cubits of the temple was three score cubits and the breadth was twenty cubits. (Threescore = 60; Cubit = 18 inches; threescore cubits = 18x60 = 1080 inches; in feet =1200/12=90 feet).

The width of the temple was twenty cubits i.e. 360 inches; in feet= 360/12= 30 feet.

Height was 30 cubits i.e. 30x18=540 inches; in feet = 540/12=45 feet.

The width of the porch in front of the main hall of the temple was 20 cubits i.e. 360 inches; in feet =30 feet; the length was equal to the breadth. The porch projected from the front of the temple and it measured 10 cubits i.e. 180 inches; in feet = 200/12 =57 feet. Solomon overlaid the entire porch with pure gold (Ref: 2 Chronicles 6:4)

Solomon made narrow windows high up in the temple walls and built side rooms against the walls of the main hall and inner sanctuary around the building. The width of the lowest floor was five cubits, and of the middle floor was six cubits and of the third floor seven cubits. He made sure that nothing could be inserted into the temple walls by making offset ledges around the outside of the temple.

There were quarries commonly called as 'Solomon's quarries' from where the stone blocks carved to shape and chiseled to fit one into another without any gap were transported to the temple site in order to see that there was no sound of any kind of took was heard at the temple site while it was being built.

The entrance to the lowest floor was on the south side of the temple. There was a stair-case from the lowest floor to the middle floor and from there to the third floor. The roof of the temple was built with beams of cedar planks. The height of side rooms that were built around the temple was five cubits and beams of cedar connected the side rooms to the temple. (Ref: 2 Chronicles 6:4-10)

According to Solomon's instructions the main hall was paneled with juniper and was covered with fine gold of "Parvaim" and decorated it with palm and chain designs. The temple was adorned with precious stones. The ceiling beams, doorframes, walls and doors of the temple were overlaid with gold and cherubim was carved on the walls.

The length and breadth of the Most Holy place of Solomon's temple was twenty cubits respectively. The inside of the Most Holy was overlaid with about 23 tons of fine gold. The gold nails that were used in the Most Holy place weighed about 1 ¼ pounds. The upper parts of the Most Holy place were overlaid with gold.

It is very interesting that Solomon made a pair of sculptured cherubim and overlaid them with gold. The span of one wing of the first cherubim was 7 ½ feet and touched temple wall on one side while the span of the other wing of the cherubim was also 7 ½ feet in length and touched wing of the pairing cherubim. Similar was the spans of the two wings of the second cherubim and one wing touched the temple wall on one side and the other the other wing of its first cherubim.

The two cherubims stood on their feet facing the main hall i.e. facing towards the Holy Place. The color of the curtain that separated the Most Holy Place and the Holy Place was of blue, purple and crimson yarn and fine linen with cherubims drawn on them.

In front of the temple Solomon erected two pillars one on either side of the temple and he called the pillar on the right side of the temple as "Jachin" and the pillar on the left side as "Boaz". Perhaps, "Jachin" means "he establishes" and "Boaz" means "in him is strength". He connected the top of these two pillars by interwoven chains that had one hundred pomegranates as in oracle of a priest.

Interestingly this comes from a passage from Exodus 28:31-35

And thou shalt make the robe of the ephod all of blue. And there shall be a hole in the top of it, in the midst thereof: it shall have a binding of woven work round about the hole of it, as it were the hole of a habergeon, that it be not rent. And beneath upon the hem of it thou shalt make pomegranates of blue, and of purple, and of scarlet, round about the hem thereof; and bells of gold between them round about:

A golden bell and a pomegranate, a golden bell and a pomegranate, upon the hem of the robe round about. And it shall be upon Aaron to minister: and his sound shall be heard when he goeth in unto the holy place before the LORD, and when he cometh out, that he die not. (Exodus 28:31-35)

CHAPTER 26
THE CONSTRUCTION DETAILS

The construction details of Solomon's Temple are mentioned in 1 Kings Chapter 7 and full chapter is quoted here below so as not to make any error.

Quote: 1 Kings 7 (NIV)

Solomon Builds His Palace

1 It took Solomon thirteen years, however, to complete the construction of his palace. 2 He built the Palace of the Forest of Lebanon a hundred cubits long, fifty wide and thirty high,[a] with four rows of cedar columns supporting trimmed cedar beams. 3 It was roofed with cedar above the beams that rested on the columns—forty-five beams, fifteen to a row. 4 Its windows were placed high in sets of three, facing each other. 5 All the doorways had rectangular frames; they were in the front part in sets of three, facing each other. [b]

6 He made a colonnade fifty cubits long and thirty wide. [c] In front of it was a portico, and in front of that were pillars and an overhanging roof.

7 He built the throne hall, the Hall of Justice, where he was to judge, and he covered it with cedar from floor to ceiling. [d] 8 And the palace in which he was to live, set farther back, was similar in design. Solomon also made a palace like this hall for Pharaoh's daughter, whom he had married.

9 All these structures, from the outside to the great courtyard and from foundation to eaves, were made of blocks of high-grade stone cut to size and smoothed on their inner and outer faces. 10 The foundations were laid with large stones of good

quality, some measuring ten cubits[e] and some eight. [f] 11 Above were high-grade stones, cut to size, and cedar beams. 12 The great courtyard was surrounded by a wall of three courses of dressed stone and one course of trimmed cedar beams, as was the inner courtyard of the temple of the Lord with its portico.

THE TEMPLE FURNISHING

13 King Solomon sent to Tyre and brought Huram,[g] 14 whose mother was a widow from the tribe of Naphtali and whose father was from Tyre and a skilled craftsman in bronze. Huram was filled with wisdom, with understanding and with knowledge to do all kinds of bronze work. He came to King Solomon and did all the work assigned to him.

15 He cast two bronze pillars, each eighteen cubits high and twelve cubits in circumference. [h] 16 He also made two capitals of cast bronze to set on the tops of the pillars; each capital was five cubits[i] high. 17 A network of interwoven chains adorned the capitals on top of the pillars, seven for each capital. 18 He made pomegranates in two rows[j] encircling each network to decorate the capitals on top of the pillars. [k] He did the same for each capital. 19 The capitals on top of the pillars in the portico were in the shape of lilies, four cubits[l] high. 20 On the capitals of both pillars, above the bowl-shaped part next to the network, were the two hundred pomegranates in rows all around. 21 He erected the pillars at the portico of the temple. The pillar to the south he named Jakin[m] and the one to the north Boaz. [n] 22 The capitals on top were in the shape of lilies. And so the work on the pillars was completed.

23 He made the Sea of cast metal, circular in shape, measuring ten cubits from rim to rim and five cubits high. It took a line of thirty cubits[o] to measure around it. 24 Below the rim, gourds

encircled it—ten to a cubit. The gourds were cast in two rows in one piece with the Sea.

25 The Sea stood on twelve bulls, three facing north, three facing west, three facing south and three facing east. The Sea rested on top of them, and their hindquarters were toward the center. 26 It was a handbreadth[p] in thickness, and its rim was like the rim of a cup, like a lily blossom. It held two thousand baths. [q]

27 He also made ten movable stands of bronze; each was four cubits long, four wide and three high. [r] 28 This is how the stands were made:

They had side panels attached to uprights. 29 On the panels between the uprights were lions, bulls and cherubim—and on the uprights as well. Above and below the lions and bulls were wreaths of hammered work. 30 Each stand had four bronze wheels with bronze axles, and each had a basin resting on four supports, cast with wreaths on each side. 31 On the inside of the stand there was an opening that had a circular frame one cubit[s] deep. This opening was round, and with its base work it measured a cubit and a half. [t] Around its opening there was engraving. The panels of the stands were square, not round. 32 The four wheels were under the panels, and the axles of the wheels were attached to the stand. The diameter of each wheel was a cubit and a half. 33 The wheels were made like chariot wheels; the axles, rims, spokes and hubs were all of cast metal.

34 Each stand had four handles, one on each corner, projecting from the stand. 35 At the top of the stand there was a circular band half a cubit[u] deep. The supports and panels were attached to the top of the stand. 36 He engraved cherubim, lions and palm trees on the surfaces of the supports and on the panels, in every available space, with wreaths all around. 37

This is the way he made the ten stands. They were all cast in the same molds and were identical in size and shape.

38 He then made ten bronze basins, each holding forty baths[v] and measuring four cubits across, one basin to go on each of the ten stands. 39 He placed five of the stands on the south side of the temple and five on the north. He placed the Sea on the south side, at the southeast corner of the temple. 40 He also made the pots[w] and shovels and sprinkling bowls.

So Huram finished all the work he had undertaken for King Solomon in the temple of the Lord:

41 the two pillars; the two bowl-shaped capitals on top of the pillars; the two sets of network decorating the two bowl-shaped capitals on top of the pillars;

42 the four hundred pomegranates for the two sets of network (two rows of pomegranates for each network decorating the bowl-shaped capitals on top of the pillars);

43 the ten stands with their ten basins;

44 the Sea and the twelve bulls under it;

45 the pots, shovels and sprinkling bowls.

All these objects that Huram made for King Solomon for the temple of the Lord were of burnished bronze. 46 The king had them cast in clay molds in the plain of the Jordan between Sukkoth and Zarethan. 47 Solomon left all these things unweighed, because there were so many; the weight of the bronze was not determined.

48 Solomon also made all the furnishings that were in the Lord's temple: the golden altar; the golden table on which was the bread of the Presence;

49 the lampstands of pure gold (five on the right and five on the left, in front of the inner sanctuary); the gold floral work and lamps and tongs;

50 the pure gold basins, wick trimmers, sprinkling bowls, dishes and censers; and the gold sockets for the doors of the innermost room, the Most Holy Place, and also for the doors of the main hall of the temple.

51 When all the work King Solomon had done for the temple of the Lord was finished, he brought in the things his father David had dedicated—the silver and gold and the furnishings—and he placed them in the treasuries of the Lord's temple.

Footnotes:

a.1 Kings 7:2 That is, about 150 feet long, 75 feet wide and 45 feet high or about 45 meters long, 23 meters wide and 14 meters high

b.1 Kings 7:5 The meaning of the Hebrew for this verse is uncertain.

c.1 Kings 7:6 That is, about 75 feet long and 45 feet wide or about 23 meters long and 14 meters wide

d.1 Kings 7:7 Vulgate and Syriac; Hebrew floor

e.1 Kings 7:10 That is, about 15 feet or about 4.5 meters; also in verse 23

f.1 Kings 7:10 That is, about 12 feet or about 3.6 meters

g.1 Kings 7:13 Hebrew Hiram, a variant of Huram; also in verses 40 and 45

h.1 Kings 7:15 That is, about 27 feet high and 18 feet in circumference or about 8.1 meters high and 5.4 meters in circumference i.1 Kings 7:16 That is, about 7 1/2 feet or about 2.3 meters; also in verse 23

j.1 Kings 7:18 Two Hebrew manuscripts and Septuagint; most Hebrew manuscripts made the pillars, and there were two rows

k.1 Kings 7:18 Many Hebrew manuscripts and Syriac; most Hebrew manuscripts pomegranates

l.1 Kings 7:19 That is, about 6 feet or about 1.8 meters; also in verse 38

m.1 Kings 7:21 Jakin probably means he establishes.

n.1 Kings 7:21 Boaz probably means in him is strength.

o.1 Kings 7:23 That is, about 45 feet or about 14 meters

p.1 Kings 7:26 That is, about 3 inches or about 7.5 centimeters

q.1 Kings 7:26 That is, about 12,000 gallons or about 44,000 liters; the Septuagint does not have this sentence.

r.1 Kings 7:27 That is, about 6 feet long and wide and about 4 1/2 feet high or about 1.8 meters long and wide and 1.4 meters high

s.1 Kings 7:31 That is, about 18 inches or about 45 centimeters

t.1 Kings 7:31 That is, about 2 1/4 feet or about 68 centimeters; also in verse 32

u.1 Kings 7:35 That is, about 9 inches or about 23 centimeters

v.1 Kings 7:38 That is, about 240 gallons or about 880 liters

w.1 Kings 7:40 Many Hebrew manuscripts, Septuagint, Syriac and Vulgate (see also verse 45 and 2 Chron. 4:11); many other Hebrew manuscripts basins

CHAPTER 27
WICKEDNESS RETURNS TO WICKED

According to the caption on Psalm 7 the psalm is written by David. In this Psalm is seen David's prayer to the LORD to save him from the curses that Cush the Benjamite hurled at him. Cush the Benjamite is identified as Shimei whose name is found in II Samuel 16:5-8

Shimei's curses hurled on David were of no small degree to be ignored of. They hit the core of the heart of the person at whom they are hurled. Hardly anybody except David would continue to hear them patiently and even allowing him to curse.

Shimei, the son of Gera, was from the family of Saul. Shimei cast stones at David and at all of his servants, all the people, and all the mighty men who were on his right hand and on his left. How daring he was that he threw stones at not only the King but also at so many others there. He could have been killed on the spot or arrested and punished later. His act seems to be one of the most foolish ones that any normal man could ever think of.

The words he uttered were so hurtful that not any man could forgive him or spare him. He said "Come out, come out, thou bloody man, and thou man of Belial" Belial means worthless man. Shimei calls King David, a chosen one of the living God, as a worthless man. (Ref: 2 Samuel 16:7). In the New Testament Paul uses this word to point to Satan (2 Corinthians 6:15). Then he cursed saying

"The LORD hath returned upon thee all the blood of the house of Saul, in whose stead thou hast reigned; and the LORD hath delivered the kingdom into the hand of Absalom thy son: and, behold, thou [art taken] in thy mischief, because thou [art] a bloody man". 2 Samuel 16:8

King David relied on God on almost everything that he did in his life but on few occasions when he did not depend on God he failed miserably. Here in this case David exhibits high degree of patience. He was the King over all Israel and was very powerful. He defeated many kings and was a man of wars and when Shimei cursed him he stood unmoved taking all the curses.

Abishai the son of Zeruiah heard the curses from Shimei and referring to him as 'dead dog' he sought permission from King David to go and take off his head but the King asked Abishai as to what he had to do with him. David went on saying that let Shimei curse him because he felt that the LORD allowed him to curse David.

David said to Abishai and to all his servants that his own son Absalom was pursing him to kill him and take over the kingdom from him. In such circumstances how would the curses from Shimei weigh more than the conspiracy of his own son Absalom?

Therefore, David allowed Shimei to curse him because he perceived that the curses were from the LORD. He probably thought that because he took over the kingdom from Saul Shiemei, a descendant from Saul, was voicing the desire of the LORD. Shimei not only cursed that the blood of the house of Saul be on David's head but also he cursed that his kingdom would be taken out from him and be given to his son Absalom.

David took refuge in the LORD and said to himself that God would show mercy on him because of his affliction and will repay him good for the curses that Shimei was pronouncing on him.

David knew that he was innocent as far as dealing with Saul and Shimei were concerned. He did not do any harm to Saul even when God delivered him into his hands. David could have killed Saul but he spared him and made him realize that his intention was not to usurp the kingdom from the anointed one, King Saul. David waited for God's will to be fulfilled and when it was time for him to be on the throne God removed Saul in His own way.

Nevertheless, he thinks that he may have inadvertently done some injustice and, therefore, prays that his enemy may overtake him if he had some fault in him. He prays to God that if he has done any iniquity or rewarded evil unto him who was at peace with him, his enemy may overtake him and persecute his soul.

"O LORD my God, if I have done this; if there be iniquity in my hands; If I have rewarded evil unto him that was at peace with me; (yea, I have delivered him that without cause is mine enemy:) Let the enemy persecute my soul, and take it; yea, let him tread down my life upon the earth, and lay mine honour in the dust. Selah" (Psalms 7:3-5)

David prays to God to arise in His anger and take vengeance against his oppressors. David was surely exhibiting a normal man's nature when he was praying to God to arise quickly and take action against his enemies; yet he waited for God's timing to come through.

David was successful in his life and very authoritative ruler over whole of Israel and yet he did not kill Shimei, who was not even equal to a small prey in his hand if he desired to kill. But without God's help Shimei would, perhaps, become a snare in his life. While he depended on God one of the five stones was enough to bring down Goliath, Philistine giant to ground. When God's strength was in David he did not need his own sword or Saul's sword or military attire to scare or kill Goliath but Goliath's sword came in handy for David to put an end to the life of Goliath the giant and his arrogance.

CHAPTER 28
DAVID PRAYS FOR JUSTICE

"My defence is of God, which saveth the upright in heart. God judgeth the righteous, and God is angry with the wicked every day" (Psalms 7:10-11)

David affirms that his defense is from God who saves the upright in heart. God surely judges the righteous according to His righteousness and grants mercy but He is angry with the wicked every day. David knew that vengeance belongs to God (Ref. Psalm 94:1). He also knew that God is merciful, gracious and slow to anger and, therefore prays to God to do justice quickly. David prays to the LORD to arise in His anger because of the rage of his enemies.

"Arise, O LORD, in thine anger, lift up thyself because of the rage of mine enemies: and awake for me to the judgment that thou hast commanded". (Psalms 7:6)

It was a prayer for his safety and the safety of the Kingdom. In Psalm 7 it was against Shimei who was cursing that David's kingdom be taken away and be given to his son Absalom, who was pursing him in a wrong way. Absalom did not do justice to his sister Tamar who was raped by Amnon, David's' son from Ahinoam, the Jezreelites. (Ref. 2 Samuel 3:2)

"And Absalom her brother said unto her, Hath Amnon thy brother been with thee? But hold now thy peace, my sister: he is thy brother; regard not this thing. So Tamar remained desolate in her brother Absalom's house" (2 Samuel 13:20)

"And David comforted Bathsheba his wife, and went in unto her, and lay with her: and she bare a son, and he called his name Solomon: and the LORD loved him". (2 Samuel 12:24)

God's providence was that the Kingdom be given to his son Solomon. Adonijah, another son of David also pursued in a wrong way to usurp the kingdom from David but God's will prevailed and Solomon became King over Israel after David.

It is to be pondered over if the curses that Shimei hurled at King David were greater than the shouting of the people before Pilate when Lord Jesus was standing before him on false charges. No! First, the chief priests and the elders persuaded the multitude to ask for the release of Barabbas, a noted criminal, in preference to Jesus. Then when Pilate was willing to release Jesus they cried saying "Crucify him, Crucify him" (Ref. Luke 23:21)

Pilate saw that his speech did not bring any fruit and, therefore, he took water, washed his hands before them and said that he was innocent of the blood of the just person but they answered and said "His blood be on us, and on our children"

"When Pilate saw that he could prevail nothing, but that rather a tumult was made, he took water, and washed his hands before the multitude, saying, I am innocent of the blood of this just person: see ye to it. Then answered all the people, and said, His blood be on us, and on our children". (Matthew 27:24-25)

As they called upon the blood of innocent Lord Jesus to be upon them and their children so it was granted to them by God. In AD 70 Roman Emperor Titus took siege of Jerusalem and killed many Jews and their children. Josephus records that a million people were killed of whom majority were Jews (Josephus, The Wars of the Jews VI.9.3)

From the cross Lord Jesus Christ prayed for their souls and for their salvation and said "...Father, forgive them; for they know not what they do... " (Luke 23:34)

CHAPTER 29
DAVID'S ADVICE

When the days of David drew near to his death he spoke to Solomon his son and charged him with few advises. First and foremost was the courage he infused in him and said to him to be strong and show himself as a man. He charged him to walk in the ways of the LORD God and to keep his commandments, his judgments and his testimonies as God gave to the children of Israel through Moses his servant.

David spoke about Joab and his shedding of blood in times of peace and made it appear as though it was a time of war. Earlier David commanded Joab to deal gently with Absalom. A man found Absalom hung from a branch of Oak tree when his long hair was caught on to the branch of the tree while he was riding a mule.

The man reported to Joab about Absalom's pathetic condition. Then, Joab questioned the man as to why he did not kill Absalom. Joab said to the man that if he had killed Absalom he would have given him ten shekels of silver and a girdle; but the man was wise enough not to incur the wrath of the King and said to Joab that even if had given him thousand shekels of silver yet would he not have killed him.

Then, Joab went ahead and thrust through the heart of Absalom three darts that he had in his hand. David charged Solomon to render justice to Joab who violated his commandment to deal gently with Absalom his son.

Those who helped in times of dire need deserved David's compassion. David recommended compassion and love for the sons of Barzilla the Gileadite who helped David and his army with food and provisions when they were returning to Jerusalem after the death of Absalom.

David did not forget to mention to Solomon about Shimie who cursed him severely when he went to Mahanaim. He said that Shimei the son of Gera who was with Solomon was not put to death by him because he swore to him that he would not kill him with the sword.

Now that Shimei was with Solomon David gave charge to Solomon to do justice and hold him not guiltless. David affirmed that Solomon was wise man and he knew how diligently Solomon would deal with Shimei.

David reined the whole of Israel for forty years and after giving full charge of the kingdom to Solomon his son, he slept with his fathers and was buried in the city of David. David was exceedingly good and he was a man with good heart. No wonder why God called him a man after His own heart.

Lord Jesus Christ gave two commandments and He demands from us that we love the Lord with all our heart, soul, and mind and with all our strength and also he demands that we love our neighbor as ourselves.

"And thou shalt love the Lord thy God with all thy heart, and with all thy soul, and with all thy mind, and with all thy strength: this is the first commandment. And the second is like, namely this, Thou shalt love thy neighbour as thyself. There is none other commandment greater than these" (Mark 12:30-31)

According to the caption on Psalm 7 the psalm is written by David. In this Psalm is seen David's prayer to the LORD to save him from the curses that Cush the Benjamite hurled at him. Cush the Benjamite is identified as Shimei whose name is found in II Samuel 16:5-8

Shimei's curses hurled on David were of no small degree to be ignored of. They hit the core of the heart of the person at whom they are hurled. Hardly anybody except David would continue to hear them patiently and even allowing him to curse.

Shimei, the son of Gera, was from the family of Saul. Shimei cast stones at David and at all of his servants, all the people, and all the mighty men who were on his right hand and on his left.

How daring he was that he threw stones at not only the King but also at so many others there. He could have been killed on the spot or arrested and punished later. His act seems to be one of the most foolish ones that any normal man could ever think of.

The words he uttered were so hurtful that not any man could forgive him or spare him. He said "Come out, come out, thou bloody man, and thou man of Belial"

Belial means worthless man. Shimei calls King David, a chosen one of the living God, as a worthless man. (Ref: 2 Samuel 16:7). In the New Testament Paul uses this word to point to Satan (2 Corinthians 6:15). Then he cursed saying

"The LORD hath returned upon thee all the blood of the house of Saul, in whose stead thou hast reigned; and the LORD hath delivered the kingdom into the hand of Absalom thy son: and, behold, thou [art taken] in thy mischief, because thou [art] a bloody man". 2 Samuel 16:8

King David relied on God on almost everything that he did in his life but on few occasions when he did not depend on God he failed miserably. Here in this case David exhibits high degree of patience. He was the King over all Israel and was very powerful. He defeated many kings and was a man of wars and when Shimei cursed him he stood unmoved taking all the curses.

Abishai the son of Zeruiah heard the curses from Shimei and referring to him as 'dead dog' he sought permission from King David to go and take off his head but the King asked Abishai as to what he had to do with him. David went on saying that let Shimei curse him because he felt that the LORD allowed him to curse David.

David said to Abishai and to all his servants that his own son Absalom was pursing him to kill him and take over the kingdom from him. In such circumstances how would the curses from Shimei weigh more than the conspiracy of his own son Absalom?

Therefore, David allowed Shimei to curse him because he perceived that the curses were from the LORD. He probably thought that because he took over the kingdom from Saul, or because he committed adultery with Bathsheba or because he conspired against Uriah and got him killed, Shiemei, a descendant from Saul, was voicing the desire of the LORD.

Shimei not only cursed that the blood of the house of Saul be on David's head but also he cursed that his kingdom would be taken out from him and be given to his son Absalom. In reality David repented of all his sins and was forgiven. However, God said sword shall not depart from his house and God's word prevailed in his life.

"Now therefore the sword shall never depart from thine house; because thou hast despised me, and hast taken the wife of Uriah the Hittite to be thy wife" (2 Samuel 12:10)

David took refuge in the LORD and said to himself that God would show mercy on him and deliver from his affliction. He consoled himself that God would be sympathetic to him rather than do harm even while Shimei was pronouncing curses on him.

David knew that he was innocent as far as dealing with Saul and Shimei were concerned. He did not do any harm to Saul even when God delivered him into his hands.

David could have killed Saul but he spared him and made him realize that his intention was not to usurp the kingdom from the anointed one, King Saul. Because Saul transgressed the command of God He chose David to be the King in his stead and David was anointed.

However, David had to wait for many years to sit on the throne as King over Israel. David waited for God's will to be fulfilled and when it was time for him to be on the throne God removed Saul in His own way.

Nevertheless, David thought that he may have inadvertently done some injustice and, therefore, prays that his enemy may overtake him if he had some fault in him. He prays to God that if he has done any iniquity or rewarded evil unto him who was at peace with him, his enemy may overtake him and persecute his soul.

"O LORD my God, if I have done this; if there be iniquity in my hands; If I have rewarded evil unto him that was at peace with me; (yea, I have delivered him that without cause is mine enemy:) Let the enemy persecute my soul, and take it; yea, let him tread down my life upon the earth, and lay mine honour in the dust. Selah" (Psalms 7:3-5)

David prays to God to arise in His anger and take vengeance against his oppressors. David was surely exhibiting a normal man's nature when he was praying to God to arise quickly and take action against his enemies.

Notwithstanding the ardent supplications he made to come upon his enemies with vengeance, yet he waited for God's timing to come through. He was successful in his life and very authoritative ruler over whole of Israel and yet he did not kill Shimei, who was not even equal to a small prey in his hand. . But without God's help Shimei would, perhaps, become a snare in his life.

While he depended on God one of the five stones was enough to bring down Goliath, Philistine giant to ground. When God's strength was in David he did not need his own sword or Saul's sword or military attire to scare or kill Goliath but Goliath's sword came in handy for David to put an end to the life of Goliath the giant and his arrogance.

CHAPTER 29
THE LORD OUR GOD IS ONE LORD

"Hear, O Israel: The LORD our God is one LORD" (Deuteronomy 6:4)

David prays to God calling on Him as "O LORD my God". This is the first time in the Psalms that David was calling the LORD as God and more so addressing individually as "my God". In Psalm 8 he calls the Lord as "O LORD our Lord".

David addresses God here in Psalm 7 individually rather than collectively and calls upon Him to render justice to him. The word in upper case as the "LORD" in KJV translation points to "Jehovah" and the word "God" points to Hebrew word "Elohiym" (Strong's definition Number 430 transliterated as "el-o-heem' " specifically used in plural sense. [And God said, Let us make man in our image, after our likeness: and let them have dominion over the fish of the sea, and over the fowl of the air, and over the cattle, and over all the earth, and over every creeping thing that creepeth upon the earth" (Genesis 1:26)]. Yet, in common parlance the word 'God' is understood to be one because God is one.

Even though God is triune He is addressed as One God. The Father, The Son and The Holy Spirit are one and they are co-equal and co-existent. They are not three Gods, but One.

In Psalm 7:1 David says that he trusted in the LORD his God. He pleads with God to save him. He prays that he may be delivered from all those who persecute him. David fears that if God does not help him his enemy would tear his soul like a lion cutting him into pieces.

Whenever enemy pursued him he sought the counsel of God and waited patiently for God to deal with the situation. He defeated Philistine Giant Goliath because he depended on God. He defeated Philistine army because he sought the will of God and followed the strategy that the LORD gave him.

Enemy might provoke us take quick decisions in opposition to what God wants us to do but when we reject the counsel of God and depend on our own strength and wisdom we will surely fail. The enemy is stronger than we are but our God is stronger than our enemy.

Peter admonishes to be sober, be vigilant because the adversary, who is Satan, comes as a roaring lion seeking whom he may devour.

"Be sober, be vigilant; because your adversary the devil, as a roaring lion, walketh about, seeking whom he may devour" (1 Peter 5:8)

When David was provoked to react to the highly abominable curses that Shimei was pronouncing on him he was not moved nor did he take pride in his strength or Kingship but allowed him to curse.

Even when Abishai said that he would take off the head of Shimei if the King permitted, David did not lose his composure. David waited for not only his entire life but even at the fag-end of his life he did not take the life of Shimei.

David handed over Shimei to the wise decision of Solomon, who was also not quick to execute Shimei but waited for Shiemei to transgress the command of the King and violate his own agreement.

Lord Jesus Christ was provoked by the mob when they mocked Him...

"...saying, Thou that destroyest the temple, and buildest it in three days, save thyself. If thou be the Son of God, come down from the cross" (Matthew 27:40)

Lord Jesus Christ who knew no sin was made sin for our sake in order that we might be made righteousness of God in Him. He died in our stead and took our punishment upon Him. Whoever believes that He is the Son of God and believes that God raised Him from the dead will be saved.

It was only one occasion that the Son of God, Lord Jesus Christ, who bore our Sin on the cross called the Father as 'My God, My God' It pleased the Father to bruise Him because He was bearing our Sin on the cross. He was forsaken by the Father when He was being judged on the cross during those three hours when darkness came upon the earth.

"For he hath made him to be sin for us, who knew no sin; that we might be made the righteousness of God in him" (2 Corinthians 5:21)

"And about the ninth hour Jesus cried with a loud voice, saying, Eli, Eli, lama sabachthani? that is to say, My God, my God, why hast thou forsaken me?" (Matthew 27:46)

CHAPTER 30
LOVE YOUR ENEMIES

David prayed to God to take quick action against Shimei but God had His own plan and David was patient for God to take action against Shimei.

David knew that the LORD shall judge people and, therefore, sought God's judgment on himself according to his righteousness and according to his integrity. He prays that the wickedness of the wicked may come to an end and establish the just (Ref. Psalms 7:8-9)

No matter how gentle and good David was, yet when it came to dealing with his adversary he prayed to God to render justice to him. He was just as any human when it came to crying to the Lord for help.

While he prayed for his deliverance from his enemy he did not allow Shiemie to go free from all that he had done to the King. David handed over Sheimie to his son Solomon to do justice according to his wisdom.

When the days of David drew near to his death he spoke to Solomon his son and charged him with few advises. First and foremost was the courage he infused in him and said to him to be strong and show himself as a man. He charged him to walk in the ways of the LORD God and to keep his commandments, his judgments and his testimonies as God gave to the children of Israel through Moses his servant.

David did not like to take action against Shimei but left for God to take vengeance.   Later while nearing his death he handed over Shimei to Solomon to deal with him according to his wisdom depending on God.

Lord Jesus Christ's prayer for his enemies was exceedingly great. Speaking on the Mount of Olives while giving his sermon on the mount he said:

"But I say unto you, Love your enemies, bless them that curse you, do good to them that hate you, and pray for them which despitefully use you, and persecute you" (Matthew 5:44)

It seems impossible in human terms to forgive enemies and love them instead. However, that is what God demands from a child of God. He desires from the child of God to bless those who curse you, and do good to them that hate you and pray for those who despitefully use you.

Lord Jesus Christ had set a good example and showed that it was possible to forgive enemies and love them. He was fully human while He was on this earth yet He was divine too. He refused to taste vinegar when He was on the cross lest His pain would subside but he bore our sin and felt the pain of the scourge and faced shame of the insults and curses that were hurled at him. He prayed for the salvation of His enemies even though He was mocked at.

The people there put on Him crown of thorns yet he did not curse any one nor did He pray to render justice to his enemies; rather he prayed to the Father to forgive them because they knew not what they were doing.

"They gave him vinegar to drink mingled with gall: and when he had tasted thereof, he would not drink" (Matthew 27:34)

"When Jesus therefore had received the vinegar, he said, It is finished: and he bowed his head, and gave up the ghost" (John 19:30)

"That if thou shalt confess with thy mouth the Lord Jesus, and shalt believe in thine heart that God hath raised him from the dead, thou shalt be saved. For with the heart man believeth unto righteousness; and with the mouth confession is made unto salvation" (Romans 10:9-10)

CHAPTER 31
THE DEATH OF SHIMEI

"Be not deceived; God is not mocked: for whatsoever a man soweth, that shall he also reap" (Galatians 6:7)

David spoke about Joab and his shedding of blood in times of peace and how he made it appear as though it was a time of war. Earlier David commanded Joab to deal gently with Absalom.

A man found Absalom hung from a branch of Oak tree when Absalom's long hair was caught on to the branch of the tree while he was riding a mule.

The man reported to Joab about Absalom's pathetic condition. Then, Joab questioned the man as to why he did not kill Absalom and he said if the man had killed Absalom he would have given him ten shekels of silver and a girdle.

The man was wise enough not to incur the wrath of the King and said to Joab that even if had given him thousand shekels of silver yet would he not have killed him. Then, Joab went ahead and thrust through the heart of Absalom three darts that he had in his hand. David charged Solomon to render justice to Joab who violated his command to deal gently with Absalom his son.

Those who helped in times of dire need deserved David's compassion. David recommended compassion and love for the sons of Barzilla the Gileadite who helped David and his army with food and provisions when they were returning to Jerusalem after the death of Absalom.

David did not forget to mention to Solomon about Shimei who cursed him severely when he went to Mahanaim. He said that Shimei the son of Gera who was with Solomon was not put to death by him because he swore to him that he would not kill him with the sword.

Now that Shimei was with Solomon David gave charge to Solomon to do justice and hold him not guiltless. David affirmed that Solomon was wise man and he knew how diligently Solomon would deal with Shimei.

David's reign on the whole of Israel was for forty years and after giving full charge of the kingdom to Solomon his son, he slept with his fathers and was buried in the city of David. David was exceedingly good and he was a man with good heart. No wonder why God called him a man after His own heart.

Solomon was dealing with every instruction intelligently and when it came to dealing with Shimei he called for Shimei and said to him to build a house for himself in Jerusalem and live there and not go anywhere.

Solomon gave freedom to Shimei to have his own house but asked him not to leave Jerusalem. He gave a stern warning that if Shimei left Jerusalem for any reason and pass the brook of Kidron he will surely be put to death and the guilt of his death would be on his own head.

Solomon was very wise king and judged every case very wisely. It was Shimei who should have taken care of himself and lived up to the desire of the King who gave ample freedom to move around Jerusalem and live in his own house.

The command from the King seemed very good to Shimei and he agreed to abide by it. Shimei lived in peace for a long while in his own house in peace and moved around freely in Jerusalem.

As the days passed by Shimei's death was also fast approaching him. It was after three years of peaceful living in Jerusalem that he faced an embarrassing situation when his two servants ran away unto Achish son of Maachah.

Achish was king of the city of Gath during the days of King David. When Shimei came to know that his two servants went to be with King Achish he left Jerusalem and went to Gath to bring back his servants.

King Solomon came to know that Shimei violated his command and left Jerusalem and went to Gath. Shimei returned to Jerusalem with his two servants.

On learning this fact the King called for Shimei and asked him if he had not made him swear by the LORD that on the day he goes out of Jerusalem he will surely be put to death and whether or not he agreed to it. Shimei had no answer to King's question. Solomon then reminded Shimei his wickedness which was in his heart when he cursed David. Solomon said that it is, therefore, that he will be put to death.

At the command of King Solomon Benewah the son of Jehoiada went and killed Shimei and the Solomon's kingdom was established. (Ref: 1 Kings 2:35-46)

CHAPTER 32
SOLOMON'S WISE DEALING

Solomon did not take hasty decision in dealing with Shimei when David handed him over to him to deal with him wisely. Even though David was a mighty King he did not kill his offender Shimei who cursed him.

Shimei was from the family of Saul and David was considerate towards him lest any should think that Saul's kingdom was forcibly taken by him or killed Shimei because he belonged to Saul's family.   It was because King Saul did not utterly destroy Amalekites that God was angry with him and took away Kingship from him and handed over it to David.

Samuel anointed David in the midst of the brethren and the Spirit of the LORD came upon him and the Spirit of the LORD departed from King Saul (Ref.! Samuel 15:15, 16:13-14) However, David started his reign when he was thirty years old and he reigned forty years. (2 Samuel 5:4)

Shimei lived peacefully for two years in Jerusalem in his own house that he built as a result of the freedom Solomon gave him but he violated King's command when he crossed over Kidron and went to Gath and brought back his two servants. Then, the King questioned Shimei as to why he did not keep the oath of the LORD and the commandment that the King charged him with.

"...Did I not make thee to swear by the LORD, and protested unto thee, saying, Know for a certain, on the day thou goest out, and walkest abroad any whither, that thou shalt surely die? and thou saidst unto me, The word that I have heard is good" 1 Kings 2:42

It was only when Shimei violated his agreement with the King that he was put to death. Solomon recounted the wickedness of Shimei and his behavior with Solomon's father David. He, then blessed his kingdom and said "throne of David shall be established before the LORD forever". After that King Solomon commanded Benaiah, the Son of Jehoida to kill Shimei and shimei was put to death.

"...king Solomon shall be blessed, and the throne of David shall be established before the LORD forever" 1 Kings 2:45

"So the king commanded Benaiah the son of Jehoiada; which went out, and fell upon him, that he died. And the kingdom was established in the hand of Solomon" (1 Kings 2:46)

The Bible emphasizes that as a man sows so does he reap and wickedness returns to the wicked. Shimei was not put to death by King David even though he had to take curses from him. King Solomon gave liberty to Shimei to have his own house and live in Jerusalem.

Shimei transgressed the command of the King and left Jerusalem, thus violating his own agreement. King David could have killed him or King Solomon could have killed him without giving him an opportunity to live freely. Shimei overstepped his freedom and left Jerusalem and brought his two servants back to Jerusalem.

Haman conspired against Mordecai and he was hung to death on the gallows that he had prepared for Mordecai.

"So they hanged Haman on the gallows that he had prepared for Mordecai. Then was the king's wrath pacified". (Esther 7:10)

Every transgressor of the commandments of the King of Kings deserves death but there is everlasting life provided for those who confess with mouth the Lord Jesus and believe in heart that God raised Him from the dead will be saved.

For the wages of sin is death; but the gift of God is eternal life through Jesus Christ our Lord. (Romans 6:23)

"That if thou shalt confess with thy mouth the Lord Jesus, and shalt believe in thine heart that God hath raised him from the dead, thou shalt be saved. For with the heart man believeth unto righteousness; and with the mouth confession is made unto salvation". (Romans 10:9-10)

CHAPTER 33
THE FALL OF SOLOMON'S KINGDOM

King Solomon's heart was right with God in the beginning of his reign as king over Israel. It was not easy for him to have the kingship over Israel inasmuch as Adonijah, David's son, had the right to become king over Israel but according to promise made by David to Bathsheba and as God desired Solomon became the king over Israel.

Solomon's reign was peaceful and he had a blessed and glorious kingdom as long as his heart was right with God. Queen Sheba appreciated the Wisdom of Solomon and the grandeur of his kingdom.

Solomon's judgment of handing over the child to its right mother was an excellent decision that was applauded by many in his kingdom. His worship with offering one thousand burnt offerings was so great and pleasing to God.

As there was no place for offering one thousand offerings at the altar he offered much of his sacrifices in the middle court, thus overstepping that which was never done, yet condoned by God at his request. His prayer of dedication of Temple was so great that it pleased one and all besides the LORD.

Yet, not before long, Solomon started gathering horses and horsemen for himself which indicated that his reliance of the Almighty God started declining. Horses, horsemen and chariots were considered as definite power of might in the Old Testament period.

Was God against gathering horses, horsemen and chariots? Yes, but did hate horses? No, the horses are his creation yet he did not allow his people to multiply them in their kingdom because relying on them for victory meant striding away from God and shunning dependence on Him. Our God is jealous LORD and He does not tolerate giving His glory to anybody else. There was instruction given to the children of Israel that when they come into the Promised Land they shall not multiply horses.

"But he shall not multiply horses to himself, nor cause the people to return to Egypt, to the end that he should multiply horses: forasmuch as the LORD hath said unto you, Ye shall henceforth return no more that way". (Deuteronomy 17:16)

Pharaoh had horses, horsemen and chariots but God drowned all of them in the Red Sea when they chased the children of Israel.

"And the waters returned, and covered the chariots, and the horsemen, and all the host of Pharaoh that came into the sea after them; there remained not so much as one of them". (Exodus 14:28)

God gave definite victory to Joshua over kings of six nations who had many horses and chariots.

"And Joshua did unto them as the LORD bade him: he houghed their horses, and burnt their chariots with fire" (Joshua 11:9)

Not only Solomon multiplied horses for himself but he married Pharaoh's daughter and later married several women from nations and had concubines. He had seven hundred wives, princesses, and three hundred concubines and they turned his heart away from God to worship Ashteroth the goddess of Zidonians, and after Milcom the abomination of the Ammonites. (Ref: 1 Kings11:1-5).

God was very angry with Solomon and, therefore, God struck Solomon with great loss. Solomon's kingdom fell very rapidly.

"Wherefore the LORD said unto Solomon, Forasmuch as this is done of thee, and thou hast not kept my covenant and my statutes, which I have commanded thee, I will surely rend the kingdom from thee, and will give it to thy servant. Notwithstanding in thy days I will not do it for David thy father's sake: but I will rend it out of the hand of thy son". (1 Kings 11:11-12)

CHAPTER 34
HORSE IS A VAIN THING FOR SAFETY

An horse is a vain thing for safety: neither shall he deliver any by his great strength. (Psalms 33:17)

Solomon worshipped at Gibeon and went to Jerusalem and reigned over all Israel. However, very early in his rule he gathered chariots and horses and horsemen and that was a sure sign that his kingdom was heading towards downfall.

The LORD God gave detailed instructions as to what the children of Israel should do when they go come into the Promised Land. Moses led the children of Israel up until the entrance of the Promised Land but because he failed in command of God he could not enter into the Promised Land.

Joshua and Caleb led the children of Israel, not those who left Egypt, but their children into the Promised Land. The Israelites who left Egypt redeemed from the bondage of Slavery under Pharaoh committed abominations displeasing the LORD and therefore, they could not enter the Promised Land as well. Their children who were born on their journey from Egypt to Canaan were led into the Promised Land by Joshua and Caleb.

The LORD foresaw the pride and disobedience of the children of Israel in the Promised Land and that they shall demand to set a king over themselves just as the nations around them would have.

The LORD said, in such circumstances the choice of setting a king shall be the one whom the LORD shall choose and one from their brethren. The LORD commanded them that no stranger would become king over them. In the same tone the LORD very firmly said that they shall not multiply horses to themselves, nor should they multiply wives for themselves or multiply for themselves gold and silver. There was reason to give such command to the children of Israel. Surely multiplying wives would turn their hearts from the LORD as also multiplying gold and silver would turn their hearts from the Him.

Lord Jesus said in Matthew 6:20 for our benefit that we should lay up treasures in heaven.

"But lay up for yourselves treasures in heaven, where neither moth nor rust doth corrupt, and where thieves do not break through nor steal" (Matthew 6:20)

Very important was the instruction that they should not multiply horses to themselves. One would wonder what the reason would be to give such a command. It was the horses and chariots that cause men to be proud of their strength.

"When thou art come unto the land which the LORD thy God giveth thee, and shalt possess it, and shalt dwell therein, and shalt say, I will set a king over me, like as all the nations that are about me; Thou shalt in any wise set him king over thee, whom the LORD thy God shall choose: one from among thy brethren shalt thou set king over thee: thou mayest not set a stranger over thee, which is not thy brother. But he shall not multiply horses to himself, nor cause the people to return to Egypt, to the end that he should multiply horses: forasmuch as the LORD hath said unto you, Ye shall henceforth return no more that way. Neither shall he multiply wives to himself that his heart turn not away: neither shall he greatly multiply to himself silver and gold". (Deuteronomy 17:14-17)

The LORD desires that His children should depend fully upon Him and not in the strength that the world offers. The horses and chariots are considered a definite strength and decisive weapons during war. However, the strength from the LORD is greater than that comes from possessing horses and Chariots.

Egyptians pursued the children of Israel, but the LORD's strength prevailed over Pharaoh's army, chariots, and horses and they were all drowned in the Red Sea. (cf. Exodus 14:9)

CHAPTER 35
HORSES AND CHARIOTS FROM EGYPT

After offering an extravagant burnt offering at Gibeon where the Tabernacle of the pattern Moses built in the wilderness was located Solomon returned to Jerusalem and not before long his reign began with full vigor his attraction was diverted to Egypt, a nation considered in the Scriptures as sinful. He gathered chariots and horsemen. He had a thousand and four hundred chariots, and twelve thousand horsemen and located chariots in the chariot cities and with the king at Jerusalem. (cf. 2 Chronicles 1:14)

Solomon not only gathered chariots, horses and horsemen but he married the daughter of Pharaoh of Egypt and there followed linen yarn, which the king's merchants received at a price. They bought a chariot for six hundred shekels or silver and horse for hundred and fifty shekels or silver from the kings of Hittites and from the kings of Syria. (One shekel was worth $10.00 in 1915 as per International Standard Bible Encyclopedia)

For Pharaoh king of Egypt had gone up, and taken Gezer, and burnt it with fire, and slain the Canaanites that dwelt in the city, and given it for a present unto his daughter, Solomon's wife. (1 Kings 9:16)

Psalmist wrote…"Some trust in chariots, and some in horses: but we will remember the name of the LORD our God" (Psalms 20:7)

"It is better to trust in the LORD than to put confidence in man. It is better to trust in the LORD than to put confidence in princes" (Psalms 118:8-9)

CHAPTER 36
SOLOMON'S TRANSGRESSION

"Thou shalt have no other gods before me" Exodus 20:3

Contrary to the commandment of the LORD that the children of Israel shall not marry women from the nations i.e. Moabites, Ammonites, Edomites, Zidonians and Hittites nor will they give their women in marriage to them Solomon loved many from those nations of which one was Pharaoh's daughter. God was very clear to the children of Israel that if they go in to them or they come in to them the nations will turn the hearts of the children of Israel to go after their gods. (Ref. 1 Kings Chapter 11)

 "And thou take of their daughters unto thy sons, and their daughters go a whoring after their gods, and make thy sons go a whoring after their gods" (Exodus 34:16)

Solomon went after Ashteroth the goddess of the Zidonians and after Milcom the abomination of the Ammonites and he did evil in the sight to the LORD.

Solomon's disobedience did not end there but he went ahead infuriating God by building high place for Chemosh, the abomination of Moab, in the hill that is before Jerusalem. How sad it is that he did this before the city on which the LORD had put His own name. He also built high place for Molech, the abomination of Amnon. His strange wives burnt incense before the idols and sacrificed unto the idols which, they worshiped, as their gods.

The result of Solomon's disobedience was seen very quickly in the fall of his kingdom.

Solomon had seven hundred wives, princess and three hundred concubines. God hates idolatry. The idolatry among those in Solomon's period was not new.

Jacob spoke the desire of the LORD when he said to his household and to all that were with him to put away the strange gods that were among them and be clean and change their garments. Earlier, Rachel stole the images that were her father's (Ref. Genesis 31:19)

"Then Jacob said unto his household, and to all that were with him, Put away the strange gods that are among you, and be clean, and change your garments" (Genesis 35:2)

"Thou shalt not make unto thee any graven image, or any likeness of anything that is in heaven above, or that is in the earth beneath, or that is in the water under the earth" (Exodus 20:4)

The defiance of the LORD's desire was seen when Aaron made a molten calf from the jewelry that he collected from the children of Israel while Moses was still on the Mount Sinai conversing with the LORD.

It is so pathetic that Aaron, who stood by Moses when miracles were shown before Pharaoh and who knew very well that it was the God of Abraham, that God of Isaac and the God of Jacob who delivered them from the bondage of slavery under Pharaoh made an image and gave it to them . The people said that it was the idol that delivered them from the bondage of slavery.

After the calf was made the children of Israel said "...These be thy gods, O Israel, which brought thee out of the land of Egypt" (Exodus 32:4). This verse should be read and understood clearly.

"And he received them at their hand, and fashioned it with a graving tool, after he had made it a molten calf: and they said,

These be thy gods, O Israel, which brought thee up out of the land of Egypt" (Exodus 32:4)

However, Aaron built an altar before it and proclaimed that the next day was the feast of the LORD and they rose up early on the morrow and offered burnt offerings and peace of offerings and rejoiced. That is a clear indication that the children of Israel did not forget Jehovah but had a misguided notion about God of heaven and the gods that they saw in Egypt. (Ref. Exodus 32:5, 6)

This is the major reason why the children of Israel were chastised number of times by God to make them understand that Jehovah is the true God.

THE LORD RAISED ADVERSARY

"And the LORD stirred up an adversary unto Solomon, Hadad the Edomite: he was of the king's seed in Edom" 1 Kings 11:14

The LORD's anger kindled against Solomon when he turned against the commandments of the LORD. The God of Israel who appeared to him twice was highly displeased with him because he transgressed the commandment of the LORD. Solomon was highly privileged and blessed King over Israel and ruled Israel for forty years.

The beginning of his reign was very peaceful and blessed. His heart was right with God when he offered thousand burnt offerings upon the altar at Gibeon (cf. 1 Kings 3:4).

After the temple was built by him at Jerusalem he offered twenty two thousand oxen and an hundred and twenty thousand sheep at the time of its dedication. The King hallowed the middle of the court that was before the LORD where these sacrifices were offered because the brazen altar that was before the LORD was too little to receive the burnt offerings, meat offerings and the fat of the peace offerings. The LORD appeared to Solomon and said to him that He heard his prayer (cf. 1 Kings 8:63-64, 2 Chronicles 7:7, 12).

As for establishing the kingdom forever the LORD put a condition. The condition was that if Solomon kept the commandments of the LORD the kingdom will have a ruler always, but if he served other gods and worshipped them then the LORD would pluck the kingdom from him by the roots and will make it to be a proverb and a byword among the nations (Ref. 2 Chronicles 7:17-20)

God appeared to Solomon first to ask him as to what God shall give unto him. Solomon asked for wisdom to go before the children of Israel, reign and judge them wisely   (cf. 1 Kings 3:5-9).

God granted Solomon's request. God appeared to him second time when Solomon finished praying to the Him at the time of dedication of the Temple that he built for Him. Solomon's prayer of dedication was very impressive and God was very much pleased with his prayer and accepted to listen to the prayers of the children of Israel who look to Jerusalem and pray provided they kept the commandments of the LORD.

Very soon Solomon drifted away from the path of the LORD the God of Israel and went after other gods as guided by his numerous wives from the prohibited nations. Then, the Lord stirred up an adversary unto Solomon, Hadad the Edomite who was of King's seed in Edom.

New Testament comes down very severely on idolatry.

Lord Jesus Christ said:

"... If any man will come after me, let him deny himself, and take up his cross, and follow me" (Matthew 16:24)

Referring to those who changed the glory of the incorruptible God into images like that of birds, four-footed beasts and creeping things.

Paul writes in Romans 1:23-26 that because they consistently refused to follow God and resorted to idolatry He gave them over to their uncleanness through the lusts of their own hearts to dishonor their own bodies, and unto women their vile affections of changing their natural use into that which is against nature and likewise to men of their vile affections of leaving the natural use of the women.

"And likewise also the men, leaving the natural use of the woman, burned in their lust one toward another; men with men working that which is unseemly, and receiving in themselves that recompense of their error which was meet" (Romans 1:27)

"Little children, keep yourselves from idols. Amen" (1 John 5:21)

"Wherefore, my dearly beloved, flee from idolatry" (1 Corinthians 10:14)

CHAPTER 37
THE ADVERSARIES OF SOLOMON

Not one but three adversaries were raised by God against King Solomon for that which he did was against the will of God. The LORD spoke to Solomon and said to him to keep His commandments and statutes but he did just the opposite.

 The LORD said to him that if he did not keep the commandments of the LORD and if he worshipped other gods the LORD would rend the kingdom from him and give it to his servant.

Notwithstanding the LORD said that He would not do it in his days because of the love that he had towards David his father. The LORD also said that He would not give the entire kingdom to his servant but will give Solomon one tribe. This was also because the LORD loved David and for the sake of Jerusalem which He chose as His city.

Solomon married several women from nations against the commandment of the LORD and he went after the desires of his wives who burnt incense to other gods. The LORD was very angry with Solomon because he went after Ashtoreth, and built high places for Chemosh, and Molech. (cf. 1 Kings 1:7-8)

In the days of David Joab the commander of the army struck down all the men in Edom but Hadad who was a child, then, fled to Egypt along with few Edomite officials.   Pharaoh gave Hadad a house to live in and provided him with food.

Later he was so pleased with him that he gave to him as his wife the sister of his own wife, whose name was Tahpenes. The sister of Tahpenes bore Hadad a son named Genubath, whom

Tahpenes brought up in the palace. Genubath had the privilege of living with Pharaoh's own children.

When Hadad heard that David was no more and Joab was also dead he sought permission from Pharaoh to let him depart and go to his own country. In spite of Pharaoh's reluctance to leave him Hadad pressed for his release from Egypt and Hadad's desire prevailed.

In the course of time it is seen how the three adversaries became snares for King Solomon.

It is God who raised adversaries against King Solomon as we read in 1 Kings Chapter 11. It is God who gave women and men to their own lusts when they resisted the will of God as we read in Romans 1:25-28.

It is God who sent Joseph ahead into Egypt to save his parents and brothers later.

"And Joseph said unto them, Fear not: for am I in the place of God? But as for you, ye thought evil against me; but God meant it unto good, to bring to pass, as it is this day, to save much people alive" (Genesis 50:19-20)

Good comes to us when we obey God and He expects from us to worship Him and acknowledge His greatness. He wants us to acknowledge that He sent His own Son, Lord Jesus Christ, into this world to save sinners. He wants to us to accept the fact that God raised Jesus from the dead on the third day.

Go d promised that no weapon formed against His children will prosper, but think at the same time when an adversary or two are raised against you, it may be because you have done something that the Lord did not desire from you (Cf. Isaiah 54:17)

"What shall we then say to these things? If God be for us, who can be against us?" (Romans 8:31)

CHAPTER 38
THREE ADVERSARIES OF SOLOMON

The LORD raised three adversaries against Solomon in consequence of the transgression he committed against the LORD and the three adversaries were:

(1) Hadad, the Edomite who was of the king's seed in Edom,

(2) Rezon the son of Eliadah, who fled from his lord Hadadezer king of Zobah, and

(3) Jeroboam the son of Nebat, who was Solomon's servant. He was an Ephrathite whose mother's name was Zeruah.

Hadad and Rezon, the two adversaries of Solomon, were like stench in the nostrils of Solomon his entire life. Hadad was a mere boy when David fought a war with Edomites and Joab the general in his army buried the dead while they were in Edom for six months. It was divine providence that Hadad escaped to Egypt along with few officials of Edom and was raised under the personal care of Pharaoh who gave in marriage his wife's sister. Hadad's son Genubeth had the privilege of playing with Pharaoh's children. Yet, when Hadad came to know that David was dead and Joab was no more, he desired to go back to Edom to take revenge on David's family. This would not have been possible if God did not allow Hadad as adversary to Solomon who transgressed the commandments of God.

Pharaoh did not know the intentions of Hadad and he reluctantly permitted Hadad to go back to Edom. Hadad failed in his attempts to fight Solomon's army stationed in several garrisons in Edom and, therefore, he sought friendship with Rezon, another adversary, whom God raised against Solomon as a consequence of his disobedience to follow statutes of God.

Earlier, Rezon fled from his lord Hadadezer, king of Zobah, and gathered men unto himself when his lord was defeated by David at Zobah (Ref. 2 Samuel 8:3).

Later Rezon became king of Damascus and "And he was an adversary to Israel all the days of Solomon, beside the mischief that Hadad did: and he abhorred Israel, and reigned over Syria" (Ref. 1 Kings 11:23-25)

The third adversary that was raised by God against Solomon was Jeroboam, who was an official in Solomon's kingdom. Solomon was very much pleased with industrious Jeroboam who was a mighty man of valor and repaired the breaches of the city of David. Solomon, therefore, set him as in charge of the entire labor force from Joseph's house.

On a day when Jeroboam was going out from Jerusalem a prophet by name Ahijah from Shiloh met him on his way and saw beautiful garment he was wearing. Ahijah took hold of the beautiful garment on Jeroboam and tore it into twelve pieces and gave ten pieces to him and said "thus saith the LORD, the God of Israel, Behold, I will rend the kingdom out of the hand of Solomon, and will give ten tribes to thee" (Ref. 1 Kings 11:31). Ahijah continued the prophecy of LORD saying...

"(But he shall have one tribe for my servant David's sake, and for Jerusalem's sake, the city which I have chosen out of all the tribes of Israel)" (1 Kings 11:32)

The prophet Ahijah spoke the word of the LORD and said that because Solomon forsook the LORD God of Israel and worshipped Ashteroth the goddess of the Zidonians. Chemosh the god of Moabities, and Milcom the god of the children of Amnon the LORD will surely rend his kingdom into two; nevertheless he will have one tribe for David whom He loved and honored saying Solomon did not keep His Statutes and judgments as did David his father.

The fulfillment of the prophesy resulted in the formation of "House of Israel" with ten tribes and "House of Judah" with two tribes (One of Judah, and another of Benjamin) with Levites who were chosen to be the priests assimilating into both the Houses.

As for New Testament believers Lord Jesus Christ gave two commandments to keep and they are:

"... Thou shalt love the Lord thy God with all thy heart, and with all thy soul, and with all thy mind. This is the first and great commandment. And the second is like unto it, Thou shalt love thy neighbour as thyself. On these two commandments hang all the law and the prophets. (Matthew 22:37-40)

It is necessary that we keep these two commandments in order that God may not turn His face from us.

"What shall we then say to these things? If God be for us, who can be against us?" (Romans 8:31)

And the opposite is true! If God is against us, who can be for us?

CHAPTER 39
SOLOMON'S KINGDOM DIVIDED

"Turn ye not unto idols, nor make to yourselves molten gods: I am the LORD your God". (Leviticus 19:4)

Throughout Bible it is seen how the LORD God of Israel, the father of our Lord Jesus Christ, was against worshipping His creation rather than the creator.

The LORD called the children of Israel as fornicators when they worshiped idols. He chastised them several times and yet they repeatedly fell into this Sin.

Solomon, who was the wisest king over Israel was no exception, and therefore, had to pay very dearly. He died after reigning as King over Israel for forty years and was buried with his fathers. In his last days Solomon wrote:

"And whatsoever mine eyes desired I kept not from them, I withheld not my heart from any joy; for my heart rejoiced in all my labour: and this was my portion of all my labour. Then I looked on all the works that my hands had wrought, and on the labour that I had laboured to do: and, behold, all was vanity and vexation of spirit, and there was no profit under the sun" (Ecclesiastes 2:10-11)

In spite of the availability of these scriptures man craves for money, position and power and seeks to fulfill fleshly desires only to realize during his last days that everything was "vanity and vexation of spirit".

It is more so if he suffers diseases consequent upon his immoral living. No doubt God forgives sin when a man asks forgiveness from God but every sin leaves behind marks in man's life and it is hard to remove them from memory. Surely God does not remember our sins after they are blotted out but Satan is very active in man's mind to bring them to memory time and again.

It was the turn of Solomon's son Rehoboam to take over as King over Israel.

Rehoboam went to Shechem where all Israel gathered to make him king.

Jeroboam, who was an official in Solomon's kingdom, was given the authority by the King over the House of Joseph and he fled to Egypt from Solomon's presence after he became adversary to Solomon in fulfillment of the LORD's prophecy. He heard the news that Israel was gathering at Shechem to make Rehoboam king over Israel and not losing much time he along with the rest of the congregation of Israel came to Shechem.

Shechem is the same place about which Stephen mentioned in Acts 7:6 about Abraham's journey via that land. It is located in Samaria, which is almost the central part of Israel, where Jacob's well was there and Lord Jesus Christ conversed with Samaritan woman (Cf. John 4:6).

Shechem is also significant inasmuch as it was the place where Jacob demanded from the children of Israel to bring their strange gods, their earrings, and he hid them under the oak tree. It was when the LORD said to Jacob to go to Bethel and dwell there and make an altar unto God. (Ref. Genesis 35:1-4)

Jeroboam spoke to Rehoboam and said that Solomon taxed the house of Joseph too much. He was pleading for tax relief because he was made in-charge by Solomon over the house of Joseph. He said if the yoke of tax is made easy on them they will serve Rehoboam forever. Rehoboam was unable to take decision immediately and gave a rash reply to Jeroboam to get back to him after three days. Jeroboam agreed and went back.

In the meanwhile Rehoboam consulted the old men who gave counsel to his father in his time. The Old men said to Rehoboam that they will be his servants forever if he answered them well and spoke good words.

The counsel of Old men did not seem good to Rehoboam and, therefore, he sought the counsel of young men of his age who grew up with him.

The counsel from the reprobate young men was so harsh and rough that their very tone was disgusting and the depraved Rehoboam accepted the young men's counsel and thwarted away the counsel from matured old men who gave counsel to his father, who was himself a wise king.

The young counselors said to Rehoboam to tell Jeroboam that his little finger shall be thicker than his father's loins and that he will chastise them with scorpions whereas, according to them, his father chastised them with whips. (Ref. 1 Kings 12:10b, 11a)

After the lapse of three days' time Jeroboam and all the people came to Shechem and sought from Rehoboam the answer to their plea.

Rehoboam answered the people in very rough tone and forsook the counsel of the old men. He spoke out the counsel that the young men of his age gave him and said…" My father made your yoke heavy, and I will add to your yoke: my father also chastised you with whips, but I will chastise you with scorpions"

All this happened in fulfillment of the prophesy of the LORD through the prophet Ahijah. It was the result of Solomon's disobedience of the LORD's commandments   and going after strange women and worshipping their gods (Ref. 1 Kings 11:29-36)

The people of Israel rebelled mightily against Rehoboam and made Jeroboam king over Northern Province. Jeroboam and the ten tribes went back with much resentment and formed their own Kingdom. As for the tribe of Judah and Benjamin they stayed with Rehoboam. Thus it was the beginning of a strong marked phase in the lives of the children of Israel.

Israel was split into two kingdoms. The northern kingdom was formed with Jeroboam as their King with ten tribes which was called the "House of Israel".

Rehoboam became the King of the Southern province which was called "House of Judah". The tribe of Levi, who were priests, mixed up on both the sides and both the houses lived at loggerheads until they were taken captive.

Northern kingdom was taken captive by the Assyrians and southern Kingdom was taken captive by the Babylonians, who later took hold of Northern Kingdom also, and thus the history of Israel is written in bloodshed.

 "And what agreement hath the temple of God with idols? for ye are the temple of the living God; as God hath said, I will dwell in them, and walk in them; and I will be their God, and they shall be my people" (2 Corinthians 6:16)

CHAPTER 40
JEROBOAM OBSTRUCTS TEMPLE WORSHIP

After the division of the Unified Israel into two kingdoms, with the Northern Province consisting of the ten tribes ruled by Jeroboam, and the Southern Province consisting of the tribe of Judah and the tribe of Benjamin ruled by Rehoboam, the tax collection by the latter posed huge burden.

Earlier, Rehoboam refused the counsel of Old matured men and did as the young men guided him resulting in the split of the Kingdom of Israel.

Rehoboam sent Adoram, who was in-charge of collecting taxes to collect tribute from the Northern Province but when the "House of Israel" saw him they stoned him to death.

King Rehoboam hurriedly escaped from the scene by getting into his chariot and fled to Jerusalem. Thereafter "House of Israel" rebelled and was at war with "House of Judah" until they were taken captive and God allowed them to remain separated until the prophecies about their unification are fulfilled (cf. Ezekiel 36, 37).

Rehoboam planned to wage war against Jeroboam but the word of the LORD came to him and to all the people of "House of Judah" that they should return to their homes and not wage war against their brethren in the Northern Province. The word of the LORD was conveyed to them by Shemaiah, the man of God. "The House of Judah" and their king Rehoboam hearkened unto the LORD's voice and obeyed.

Jeroboam built Shechem in mount Ephraim, and lived there and went out from there and built Penuel. (Shechem was destroyed by Abimelech (cf. Judges 9:1-49), and Penuel was a ruined city (cf. Judges 8:9)).

Jeroboam faced a great dilemma as to how to avoid his people to go to Jerusalem every year to celebrate Passover festival. Jerusalem was in the southern province and his people were in the Northern Province and their people had to necessarily travel to Jerusalem to celebrate Passover festival.

Keeping the Passover festival was mandatory as the LORD commanded them to do. Jeroboam was convinced in his heart that if the people from his kingdom went to Jerusalem and worshipped God at Jerusalem they would not return to his kingdom and accept Rehoboam as their king, thus putting his own position in a very awkward situation.

As Satan would have his day when men face with dilemma the Old Dragon, the one that cheated Adam and Eve in the Garden of Eden, was very active and impoverished the brain of Jeroboam with wicked thoughts. Jeroboam soon developed a scheme to avoid his people to travel to Jerusalem.

It is so true even in these days that the adversary, who was the cheater from the beginning, makes men busybodies and constrains them to avoid places of worship, where they usually worship the living God.

Jeroboam quickly devised a plan and made two calves of gold and said to his people that it is too arduous a task for them to travel to Jerusalem to offer sacrifices; instead they would well sacrifice to the idols, which he called them as their gods who brought them out of the land of Egypt. He set up one idol at Bethel and the other at Dan. He appointed priests of the lowest standard and those who were not the sons of Levi.

Bethel was at the border delineating his Province from that of Southern Province and Dan was the northern border. This became a sin which the LORD abhorred. The people from his kingdom went even unto Dan to worship the idols.

Jeroboam ordained a feast on the fifteenth day of the eight month just as the "House of Judah" celebrated but he and his people offered sacrifices to idols at Dan and Bethel and offered incense to them. They did just opposite to what the LORD commanded them to do and that was the beginning of the fall of the "House of Israel".

When Jesus was tempted by the devil in the wilderness to make the stones into bread after he had fasted for forty days and forty nights and when he was hungry he sternly replied ...

"It is written, Man shall not live by bread alone, but by every word that proceedeth out of the mouth of God"

Then, the devil took him to the pinnacle of the temple and tempted to cast Himself down and quoted a Scripture but the Lord said...

"... It is written again, Thou shalt not tempt the Lord thy God"

Again the devil took Jesus to an exceedingly high mountain and showed Him the kingdoms of the world and the glory of them and said that he would give all of them to Jesus, the Lord replied.

"Get thee hence, Satan: for it is written, Thou shalt worship the Lord thy God, and him only shalt thou serve" (cf. Matthew 4:1-10)

No matter who sets up idols in our lives and force us to worship them it is very essential that we worship the living God, the father of our Lord Jesus Christ and Him only.

CHAPTER 41
HEZEKIAH DEFEATS SENNACHERIB

Out of twenty kings of the Kingdom of Judah there were only few kings who did that which was right in the sight of the LORD. One of them was King Hezekiah.

There was none before him in the history of kings of Judah who trusted and revered the LORD so much as he did. He was twenty five years old when he began to reign and reigned for twenty nine years in Jerusalem. The LORD was with him and he prospered.

"He removed the high places, and brake the images, and cut down the groves, and brake in pieces the brasen serpent that Moses had made: for unto those days the children of Israel did burn incense to it: and he called it Nehushtan" (2 Kings 18:4)

Hezekiah rebelled against King of Assyria and did not serve him and defeated Philistines. In his fourth year of reign Shalmaneser, king of Assyria, attacked Samaria, besieged it took full control of it in two years. He took captive of Israel and moved them to Halah, Habor and to the cities of Medes.

The LORD gave them over to King of Assyria because they transgressed God's covenant and were disobedient to the Laws gives by God through His servant Moses.

Sennacherib, king of Assyria came up against Hezekiah in the fourteenth year of latter's reign and fenced cities of Judah and took them. Lachish was a very strategic city where the armies pitch one against another for war and it is at that city that Sennacherib came boasted in pride.

Hezekiah, king of Judah, was depressed and disappointed and, therefore, sent word of apology that would take punishment for not serving him. Sennacherib imposed on Hezekiah a fine of three hundred talents of silver and thirty talents of gold, which was huge sum.

Hezekiah raised the sum from the house of the Lord, treasures of the king's house and even from the gold from the doors of the Solomon's temple and gave to it king Sennacherib.

It is very strange that a king, who had so much faith in God and who did right in the sight of the LORD and trusted the LORD more than anyone in the Kingdom of Judah did before him, now getting disappointed when faced with some trying situation such as Sennacherib taking over Lachish and cities of Judah. Rightly so, he showed that he was also fallible and human just as any of us.

Elijah, who was so courageous a prophet, once feared Jezebel and ran from her presence to hide himself, but later recovered from that fear when the angel of the LORD comforted him. He heard the voice of the LORD not in strong wind, or in the earthquake, or fire, but in a still small voice that said "What doest thou here, Elijah" and Elijah obeyed the instructions from the LORD (1 Kings 19-4-14)

Likewise, King Hezekiah also recovered from fear and brought Sennacherib to his feet when God helped him consequent upon his praying to the LORD for help. Sennacherib's blasphemous words, arrogant speech came to nothing.

Sennacherib sent Tartan, Rabsaris and Rabshakeh from Lachish to Hezekiah and they stood by the conduit of the upper poor and spoke to Eliakim and Shebna, and Joah of Hezekiah's representatives and insulted them and questioned them as to who would or which God could save them from his attack.

Rabshakeh cried with a loud voice in Jewish language saying Hezekiah's God cannot save the people of Judah and said to them to make agreement with king of Assyria but he people held peace at the command of Hezekiah.

Rabshakeh told the king Hezekiah about the blasphemous words that Rabshakeh spoke at the instance of Sennacherib and it made Hezekiah a grievous man.

King Hezekiah rent his clothes, covered himself in sackcloth and went to the LORD for help. Isaiah heard about Hezekiah's concern and conveyed to him message that "Thus saith the LORD, Be not afraid of the words which thou hast heard, with which the servants of the king of Assyria have blasphemed me".

Hezekiah prayed to the LORD saying "O LORD God of Israel, which dwellest between the cherubims, thou art the God, even thou alone, of all the kingdoms of the earth; thou hast made heaven and earth".

The LORD heard prayer of Hezekiah and the angel of the LORD went out and "smote in the camp of the Assyrians an hundred fourscore and five thousand: and when they arose early in the morning, behold, they were all dead corpses". (1 Kings 19:35)

Sennacherib, king of Assyria, went back and lived in Nineveh and worshipped his god, Nisroch and he was killed by his own two sons. (cf. 2 Kings 19:36-37)

Later when Hezekiah fell sick unto death Isaiah the prophet said to him to pray to the LORD for help and when Hezekiah prayed to the LORD his life was extended by fifteen years and he reigned successfully for fifteen more years and slept with his fathers and Manasseh reigned in his stead.

God is our rock of refuge and He helps us in all situations, whether they be small or trying situations when we seek His help.

"But the LORD is my defence; and my God is the rock of my refuge" (Psalms 94:22)

CHAPTER 42
PASSIONS RUN HIGH

"And he said unto him, I am the LORD that brought thee out of Ur of the Chaldees, to give thee this land to inherit it" (Genesis 15:7)

Beliefs and passions run very high and deep in the land of Israel because it is the land of three great faiths – Judaism, Christianity and Islam. The history of Israel is so complicated and contentious and, therefore, as Christians, it is apt that we depend on what is recorded in the Bible rather than any history book.

The whole of land of Israel is said to be not greater than New Jersey or even half of Georgia State where I live, yet the land of Israel is known to have suffered with wars and disputes.

The disputes can be traced back even unto the days of Abraham, who was also known as 'father Abraham' by all the three faiths. Abraham's name was "Abram" before he was renamed by God as "Abraham".

A covenant is a mutual agreement between two parties and it is deemed to have agreed upon when both the parties pass between the divided pieces of an animal that are laid against each other indicating that if any one of the party breaks the covenant his body would suffer the same death as the animal suffered. There are two types of covenants recorded in the Bible and they are

1.   Conditional and

2.   Unconditional

The covenant that God made with Abraham was Unconditional. The LORD said to Abram to take an heifer of three years old, a she goat of three years old, a ram of three years old, turtle dove and a young pigeon and divide them in the midst and lay each piece one against another. Abram did as the LORD commanded him. He did not divide birds and when the fowls came down on the carcasses, he drove them away (Ref. Genesis 15:7-11)

As the dusk started growing a deep sleep fell upon Abram and lo, a horror of great darkness fell upon him. The LORD spoke to Abram in his sleep and said to be sure that His seed shall be stranger in the land that is not theirs and shall serve the nation which will afflict them for four hundred years and that the LORD will judge that nation.

As a seal affixed to the covenant by the LORD the burning lamp of the LORD passed between those pieces. It may be noted here that Abram did not pass between the divided pieces which clearly indicates that it was one sided agreement.

In the same day the LORD made a covenant with Abram that He gave the land to him from the river of Egypt unto the great river, the river Euphrates; this land is commonly called as the "fertile crescent".

Obviously, as seen in the Scriptures the word of the LORD with regard to their bondage of slavery was fulfilled when the children of Israel served Pharaoh of Egypt for four hundred years and, thereafter, God judged Pharaoh and Egypt.

The covenant that was made between God and Moses was conditional, that is to say, if they did what the LORD said to them, then God would do what He promised to them.

However, the covenant that the LORD made with Abram was one sided, that is, the LORD made the covenant with Abram and He will fulfill His covenant no matter what the seed of Abram would do. God's promise will never fail and He will not go back on anyone of His promises. The LORD's covenant with Abram was from the LORD and He did not put a condition to fulfill His promise. (Ref. Genesis Chapter 15)

The LORD said to Abram as we read in Genesis Chapter 17 that he shall circumcise the flesh of his foreskin and it shall be a token of the covenant. He also said that every male of eight days old shall be circumcised among his people.

Whoever did not obey this command of the LORD was cut off from the lineage of Abram but still the covenant the LORD made with Abram was not treated as abrogated.

The LORD's Promise still stands to be fulfilled in the lives of the descendants of Abraham. The LORD gave privilege to those who are bought with money by Abram and his descendants to reap the blessings of Abram when they are circumcised and otherwise they do not. (Ref. Genesis 17:11-14)

New Testament believer can be sure that it is not by keeping the Law of Moses that the promises are inherited but by the promise that the LORD made to Abraham (Cf. Galatians 4:7, Romans 8:17, Romans 10:17, Ephesians 2:8)

"For if the inheritance be of the law, it is no more of promise: but God gave it to Abraham by promise" (Galatians 3:18)

"For with the heart man believeth unto righteousness; and with the mouth confession is made unto salvation" (Romans 10:10)

CHAPTER 43
CIRCUMCISION PROFITS NOTHING

"And he gave him the covenant of circumcision: and so Abraham begat Isaac, and circumcised him the eighth day; and Isaac begat Jacob; and Jacob begat the twelve patriarchs". (Acts 7:8)

Admonishing Galatians time and again, Apostle Paul continues to emphasize on the fact that there is salvation only in Jesus through faith by grace and not by law and works associated with it.

Getting entangled with law and with the thought that they need to do something to be saved, is tantamount to be under the yoke of bondage.

About circumcision he condemns it and says that if anyone is of the belief that circumcision is necessary for salvation or for justification, the obsession of such thought will not profit them and Christ and his blood is of nothing to them.

Everyone, who is circumcised, becomes debtor to the whole law and Christ and his sacrifice has nothing for him. We are reckoned as righteous only by faith in Jesus and by his grace. Neither circumcision nor un-circumcision avails anything to a believer in Christ

While giving an answer to the high priest Stephen says that Abraham circumcised Isaac on the eighth day in compliance to the covenant that existed between God and him. It continued in the Old Testament among the children of Israel.

But during the period of Acts of the Apostles when Peter was speaking the Holy Spirit was poured out on the Gentiles as well.

The Jews who were circumcised were surprised to see that on the Gentiles also the gift of the Holy Spirit was poured.

"And they of the circumcision which believed were astonished, as many as came with Peter, because that on the Gentiles also was poured out the gift of the Holy Ghost". (Acts 10:45)

As we read through Acts 11th Chapter we see that Peter was accused of joining with Gentiles but then he expounded to them as to how God revealed to him that he should not treat unclean that which God has cleansed. (Acts 11:9)

In Romans Chapter 2 Paul condemns the thought that circumcision can save a person. (Romans 2:27-29)

Walking in the Spirit and hatred of lust of the flesh are necessary on the part of a believer to lead a holy life. One great truth a believer has to understand is that flesh lusts against the Spirit and the Spirit against the flesh and these are contrary to each other. If we are of the Spirit and are led by the Spirit we are not under the law and would not yield to the desires of the flesh.

After having known of the love of God through His one and only begotten son, Jesus, why would we turn yet unto beggarly elements like observing the days, months, times and years, and be subject again to be under the bondage of the law?

When the price for our sin and redemption is already paid for, why would we turn again to work for our salvation by ourselves? Salvation is available free of cost; the price is already paid for.

All that is needed on the part of sinner is to believe that Jesus paid the price of his sin on the cross, and that he needs to believe in his heart this fact and accept him as his personal Savior.

Apostle Paul blesses those, who do not voluntarily subject themselves to be under the yoke of law, but accept Christ's death upon the cross. He says fulfilling the law of Christ is more important than that of the Old Testament laws.

No one should boast of himself or glory himself but everyone should glorify Lord Jesus Christ, whose marks were borne by not only Apostle Paul but all those, who realize the efficacy of the blood of Lord Jesus Christ.

"For circumcision verily profiteth, if thou keep the law: but if thou be a breaker of the law, thy circumcision is made uncircumcision". (Romans 2:25)

CHAPTER 44
THE TEMPLE DESTROYED

King Jeroboam and his successors did evil in the sight of the LORD. Nineteen Kings ruled the Northern Kingdom and there was not a single one of them, who did what was pleasing to the LORD.

They all, one after another, did evil in the sight of the LORD and deviated from God's ways and followed after their own methods by setting up idols and burning incense to them. Therefore, the Northern Province, which was the "House of Israel", incurred the wrath of God.

The LORD handed over them to Assyrian King, who conquered the Northern Kingdom and took captive of "House of Israel" and scattered them.

The Assyrian king's strategy was to relocate them in different regions in order that they might not become united to rebel against him.

In the ninth year of Hoshea the king of Assyria took Samaria, and carried Israel away into Assyria, and placed them in Halah and in Habor by the river of Gozan, and in the cities of the Medes" (2 Kings 17:6)

"Until the LORD removed Israel out of his sight, as he had said by all his servants the prophets. So was Israel carried away out of their own land to Assyria unto this day". (2 Kings 17:23)

Thus the 'House of Israel' was scattered and, in spite of many Jews returning to Israel during Persian Regime, and in subsequent periods of time, and even after Israel becoming one

Nation on 14th May, 1948, no one until today is able to locate them fully as to where they are.

Before Solomon fell from the presence of God he married Pharaoh's daughter and built a separate palace for her (Ref. 1 Kings 3:1, 9:24).

The LORD's anger burnt first against Solomon, next against Rehoboam, and then against Jeroboam. Solomon's glorious Temple, inside of which was fully overlaid with gold, was looted by Shishak, King of Egypt, in the fifth year of King Rehoboam.

"And it came to pass in the fifth year of king Rehoboam, that Shishak king of Egypt came up against Jerusalem; And he took away the treasures of the house of the LORD, and the treasures of the king's house; he even took away all: and he took away all the shields of gold which Solomon had made."(1 Kings 14:25, 26)

As for Southern Kingdom, there were only some of the Kings, of the total twenty Kings, who obeyed God fully and others did the same as their brethren in the Northern Kingdom.

Babylonians took captive of Southern Kingdom and they destroyed the Temple. Later Babylonians subdued Assyrians and the rest is history.

Solomon's Temple was rebuilt as authorized by Cyrus but that was not as elegant as the first temple was. It did not last long after Lord Jesus Christ's death, resurrection and ascension. When Jesus was facing trial before Pilate he was found not guilty of any crime, yet the people cried that He should be crucified.

Pilate saw that he could not prevail upon them to ask for the release of Jesus, he took water and washed his hands before the multitude, saying "I am innocent of the blood of this just person: see ye to it. Then answered all the people, and said, His blood be on us, and on our children" (Ref. Matthew 27:24b-25)

Neither Pilate, who as a governor with earthly authority, released nor the people there preferred Jesus to be released instead of noted criminal Barabbas; rather they vehemently cried that He should be crucified.

They answered and said "His blood be on us, and on our children". They, indeed, paid very dearly in AD 70 when Roman army under Titus, son of Emperor Vespasian, sieged Jerusalem and destroyed the Temple utterly and leveled it to the ground fulfilling the prophecy of Lord Jesus Christ.

"And Jesus went out, and departed from the temple: and his disciples came to him for to shew him the buildings of the temple. And Jesus said unto them, See ye not all these things? verily I say unto you, There shall not be left here one stone upon another that shall not be thrown down". (Matthew 24:1-2)

God was so unapproachable and terrible in the Old Testament period and He punished other nations for the sake of protecting and blessing His children but whenever His people worshipped other gods he chastised them terribly.

One King after another fell beyond recognition and the glorious temple built by Solomon was destroyed. The second temple was leveled to the ground leaving not a single stone one upon another.

It is, indeed, so terrible to dishonor God and worship other gods behind the idols. Somehow man seems to be hankering after finding peace and solace in the faces of idols that do not speak, nor hear. But there is real peace and joy in worshipping the Lord in spirit and in truth. Lord Jesus Christ said He is the way, the truth and the life.

Jesus saith unto him, I am the way, the truth, and the life: no man cometh unto the Father, but by me. (John 14:6)

Peter, one of the disciples said:

"Neither is there salvation in any other: for there is none other name under heaven given among men, whereby we must be saved". (Acts 4:12)

Believe in Lord Jesus Christ. Today is the day of salvation.

CHAPTER 45
SOLOMON'S RESTORATION

In the Bible we come across several stalwarts of faith and followers of God erring in their daily lives. It is not uncommon that men fell into sin and were forgiven of God. Some of those who fell from the presence of God and made lasting impression on mankind are as follows:

Adam and Eve transgressed the commandment of God who said to them that they should not eat of the fruit of the tree of the knowledge of good and evil and passed on their Sin to entire mankind. Their folly resulted in knowing that they were naked and needed a covering for their body. Their own efforts of providing covering for their bodies were found short of God's requirements and, therefore, God clothed them with coats of skins. (Ref. Genesis 2:17, 3:21)

Abraham, who was called as man of faith, faltered on one occasion when he said to his wife that she should say that she was his sister when they journeyed toward Gerar. Abimelech, king of Gerar took Sarah, but God intervened and no harm was done to Sarah. (Ref. Genesis 20:1-2)

Moses, the faithful servant of the LORD, faltered once when he struck the rock for water instead of speaking to it, and God did not permit him to enter the Promised Land in spite of his ardent prayer request that he may be allowed to see the Promised Land and yet he was found with Lord Jesus Christ during His transfiguration.

"I pray thee, let me go over, and see the good land that [is] beyond Jordan, that goodly mountain, and Lebanon.

However, the LORD was wroth with me for your sakes, and would not hear me: and the LORD said unto me, Let it suffice thee; speak no more unto me of this matter". Deuteronomy 3:25-26

"And after six days Jesus taketh Peter, James, and John his brother, and bringeth them up into a high mountain apart, and was transfigured before them: and his face did shine as the sun, and his raiment was white as the light. And, behold, there appeared unto them Moses and Elias talking with him". Matthew 17:1-3

David committed adultery with Bathsheba and got her husband killed and yet when he repented God forgave him.

THERE IS FORGIVENESS

The second malefactor on the cross said a simple prayer and Lord Jesus Christ was gracious to him.

"And he said unto Jesus, Lord, remember me when thou comest into thy kingdom. And Jesus said unto him, Verily I say unto thee, To day shalt thou be with me in paradise. Luke 23:42, 43

In the case of Solomon's transgression there was a provision made by God when He said to David that he will chasten him with the rod of men and with the stripes of the children of men but His mercy shall not depart from him. (Ref. 2 Samuel 7:13-15). In addition, many verses from the book of Song of Solomon and the Book of Ecclesiastes; especially the last two verses from the Book of Euclasites reveal that Solomon repented.

"Let us hear the conclusion of the whole matter: Fear God, and keep his commandments: for this [is] the whole [duty] of man. For God shall bring every work into judgment, with every secret thing, whether [it be] good, or whether [it be] evil". Ecclesiastes 12:13-14

In the light of the above facts it can be safely concluded that Solomon is saved by the grace of God.

CHAPTER 46
LOOKING UNTO JESUS

"Looking unto Jesus the author and finisher of our faith; who for the joy that was set before him endured the cross, despising the shame, and is set down at the right hand of the throne of God" (Hebrews 12:2)

"But I have chosen Jerusalem, that my name might be there; and have chosen David to be over my people Israel". 2 Chronicles 6:6

King David enjoyed this privilege and being the king over all Israel and likewise King Solomon enjoyed this privilege. They had such great power given by the LORD that no one could raise any voice against them. King Solomon had compassion and set Adonijah his brother free from being killed of the charges of conspiracy against him, but when Adonijah desired to have Abishag, a concubine of David, after the death of David as his wife. Solomon was furious and ordered Adonijah's execution.

Solomon's prayer of dedication of Temple was so impressive. So great was King Solomon with absolute power, yet when it came to praying to God he humbled and stood on the brass platform. He did not have a seat there on the platform and he lifted up his voice to God with his hands stretched praying for the people of Israel. Solomon's heart was right before God in his initial days.

Solomon realized that the temple he built for the LORD cannot contain Him because the heaven is His throne and the earth is His footstool and He acknowledges that he was a servant of the LORD and submits his supplications and intercessory prayer to the LORD saying that He may have resect to Solomon's prayer.

The content of his prayer is to be noted very carefully. Solomon prays to the LORD to keep His eyes open day and night upon the 'House of the LORD' he built because the LORD had put His name on it.

The details of intercessory of prayer of Solomon are worthy to ponder on.   There is no reason, according to me, that Solomon lost his salvation.

According to Bible there is no one on the face of the earth who had not committed sin; all have sinned and come short of the glory of God.

The wages of sin is death but the gift of God is everlasting life. Solomon had to pay very dearly for all the sins he committed. His kingdom was rent into two. Yet, Solomon's turning to other gods was a not a permanent one; but as is evident from other references in the Bible it can be safely concluded that he repented of his sin.

CHAPTER 47
FATHER FORGIVE THEM

"I have manifested thy name unto the men which thou gavest me out of the world: thine they were, and thou gavest them me; and they have kept thy word" (John 17:6)

The intercessory prayer recorded in John Chapter 17 is indeed great. There are few similarities seen in the intercessory prayers of Moses and Lord Jesus Christ, yet Moses was human and Lord Jesus Christ is the "Son of God".

Moses was son of Hebrew Parents, of the tribe of Levi. He chose a life of hardship in order to save God's chosen people, his own kinsmen, Israelites.

Moses escaped the wrath of Pharaoh, when he chose to rescue his brethren. His life span lasted for 120 years, divided in to forty equal parts of very fruitful years.

First set of forty years were of his growth from his childhood to an young man, second set of forty years constituted his earthly life, third set of forty years forty years were dedicated by him for the deliverance of his own brethren, from the bondage of slavery under Pharaoh, and led them to the Promised land of Canaan.

He became leader after eighty years and spent forty years of fruitful years as a leader; nevertheless he once took his own decision outside the will of God resulting in being denied to enter into the Promised Land.

"Because ye trespassed against me among the children of Israel at the waters of Meribah-Kadesh, in the wilderness of Zin; because ye sanctified me not in the midst of the children of

Israel. Yet thou shalt see the land before thee; but thou shalt not go thither unto the land which I give the children of Israel" (Deuteronomy 32:51-52)

It was to enter the promised land of Canaan, which was denied to him, because of his choice of making his own will prevail upon God's will.

God wrote the Ten Commandments on two tablets with his own finger and gave to Moses to deliver them to the children of Israel but when he came down from Mount Sinai after having direct conversation with God he saw the children of God worshipping idols of manmade gods.

Moses got furious and broke down the tablets containing the Ten Commandments. Once he struck the rock to fetch water at "Horeb" according to God's will but next time in order to fetch water in the wilderness of Zin, he took his own decision of striking the rock instead of speaking to it (Ref: Numbers 20:8, 11)

God gave him second time, the same Ten Commandments, which he preserved in the 'Tabernacle'. Moses wrote Torah, which constituted the five books, namely, Genesis, Exodus, Leviticus, Numbers and Deuteronomy. Moses died a natural death.

"Giving thanks unto the Father, which hath made us meet to be partakers of the inheritance of the saints in light: Who hath delivered us from the power of darkness, and hath translated us into the kingdom of his dear Son: In whom we have redemption through his blood, even the forgiveness of sins: Who is the image of the invisible God, the firstborn of every creature" (Colossians 1:12-15)

Lord Jesus Christ was the 'Lamb of God' as John the Baptist pointed in John 1:36 and he was without any blemish

(Ephesians 5:27, 1 Peter 1:19) and He was without any sin (Hebrews 4:15) and yet it pleased the Father to bruise Him for our sins (Isaiah 53:10) and was made to be sin for us that we might be made the righteousness of God in Him (2 Corinthians 5:21)

Lord Jesus Christ prayed for forgiveness of the very people who were crucifying him and He forgives the sins of everyone who confesses his sins to Him...

"Then said Jesus, Father, forgive them; for they know not what they do. And they parted his raiment, and cast lots" (Luke 23:34)

CHAPTER 48
WORSHIP THE LORD

WORSHIP HIM IN SPIRIT AND IN TRUTH

"God is a Spirit: and they that worship him must worship him in spirit and in truth". (John 4:24)

If it is not because of the love of God towards us we would have been consumed long ago. When we consider the stars, moon, and the Sun in the sky what is man that God should think of us. After all we are made of dust and dust that we are we will return to dust; but there is great hope for us, who believe in Christ, that we will have everlasting life and will be immortal.

Any creation that is seen regularly by man for quite some would take the form of an idol in his mind. He would pay too much attention to it until he finds that there is no hope in it but there is hope only in the Creator.

Man has tendency to make idols of even the things that are given for his benefit and soon starts worshipping them. God demands from men that they give pre-eminence to Him in everything and worship Him and none else. The LORD said that He will not give His glory to anyone else.

"I am the LORD: that is my name: and my glory will I not give to another, neither my praise to graven images" (Isaiah 42:8)

As the children of Israel journeyed from mount Hor by the way of the Red sea to encircle the land of Edom they were tired greatly and they spoke against God and their leader Moses. They questioned Moses as to why he brought them out of Egypt and if it was for them to die in the wilderness because they did not find bread or water there; they hated the heavenly bread, "Manna".

The LORD chastised them even unto death of many, who were bitten by fiery snakes sent by Him among them. The people realized that they sinned and went to Moses and confessed that they have sinned by speaking against the LORD and against Moses. They requested Moses to pray unto the LORD that he may take away the serpents from them and Moses prayed.

At the intercession of Moses God provided a way and according to His instructions he made a serpent of brass and set it upon a pole. Anyone, who was bitten by serpent, looked at the brass serpent lifted by Moses, lived. (Ref. Numbers 21:4-9)

The metal brass in the Scriptures indicates judgment. Similar to such brazen serpent raised in the wilderness by Moses, it was on the cross that Lord Jesus Christ, who was in the form of man, was lifted up and our sin on Him was judged.

The shadow of the things that were to be fulfilled in Jesus was seen in the form of brazen serpent in the wilderness. Lord Jesus Christ, who knew no sin, was made sin for our sake and suffered death even unto death on the cross.

We remember the death of Lord Jesus Christ who is unseen yet felt by us in our spirit. We worship Him in spirit and in truth and we are not instructed to make His mages nor are we instructed to burn incense to Him

No earthly building can contain Him. The heaven is His throne and earth is footstool. We are so privileged and blessed that the Lord, who is so great, dwells in our hearts.

As the brazen serpent remained as relic among the children of Israel for many years they had gone to extreme and worshipped and burnt incense to it. It was Hezekiah, one of the Kings of

Judah who was bold enough to treat it as nothing but a piece of brass and removed from among them not only the high places and broke the images, cut down the groves, but also broke the brass serpent into pieces thus ending abhorrent worship of idols. .

"He removed the high places, and brake the images, and cut down the groves, and brake in pieces the brasen serpent that Moses had made: for unto those days the children of Israel did burn incense to it: and he called it Nehushtan" 2 Kings 18:4

"For God so loved the world that he gave his only begotten Son, that whosoever believeth in him should not perish, but have everlasting life". (John 3:16)

CHAPTER 35
CROWN OF RIGHTEOUSNESS

"I have fought a good fight, I have finished my course, I have kept the faith: Henceforth there is laid up for me a crown of righteousness, which the Lord, the righteous judge, shall give me at that day: and not to me only, but unto all them also that love his appearing". (2 Timothy 4:7-8)

At the fag-end of Paul's life when he knew that he would not live anymore, because of his impending execution unto death by Nero for preaching the Gospel, he writes letter to Timothy, whom he called as his son in faith and in Christian ministry, exhorting him to preach the word of God. He recollects his own ministry and says that he fought a good fight, finished his course, and kept the faith.

Paul, therefore, says that the Lord Jesus Christ will give him a crown of righteousness at the Judgment seat of Christ. He says not only he receives such crown of righteousness but all those who believe in Lord Jesus Christ and love His second coming.

Indeed, Paul struggled hard to proclaim the Gospel of Lord Jesus Christ from the beginning of his ministry. He had a bad past record of persecuting Christians.

Paul's name was Saul before his conversion to Christianity. He had consented to the death of Spirit-filled Stephen and kept the raiment of them that slew him.   He threatened to slaughter the disciples of the Lord. He desired letters from high priest to Damascus to the synagogues that if he found any disciples of the Lord, whether be men or women, he would bring them bound to Jerusalem.

However, as he journeyed to Damascus he encountered Lord Jesus Christ on the way. There shone a great light suddenly from heaven around him. Saul fell down to the ground and he heard a voice asking him "Saul, Saul, why persecutest thou me?" Saul answered and said "Who are thou Lord?" Then the Lord answered him and said "I am Jesus whom thou pesecutest: it is hard for thee to kick against pricks".

It is indeed hard to be obstructive, or stubborn not to believe Jesus as the Lord and fight against His teachings. The ox that kicks against pricks hurts itself and none else. The pricks refereed to here are goads that the farmer uses to prick the ox while farming. The stubborn ox that kicks against such goads, which are sharp iron pieces stuck into the edge of the stick, injures itself and none else.

The Lord was using this phrase against Saul who was persecuting Christians and the disciples. Hurting Christians was like hurting Lord Jesus Christ Himself. Saul was thrown onto the ground and humbled in no time and was made blind. The voice from Lord Jesus Christ was heard by others who were accompanying Saul but they could not see any man. Saul humbled himself immediately.

 It is the obedience and change of heart that God demands at a man's conversion to follow Jesus. Then there should be the willingness to accept Lord Jesus Christ as savior. Confessing by mouth the Lord Jesus Christ and believing in heart that God raised Him from the dead will earn salvation and that is called 'born-again'. The salvation is neither earned by gold nor silver or good works but by faith in Him alone.

"That if thou shalt confess with thy mouth the Lord Jesus, and shalt believe in thine heart that God hath raised him from the dead, thou shalt be saved" (Romans 10:9).

When Lord Jesus Christ was on this earth Nicodemus, a ruler of Jews, who saw the miracles that the Lord Jesus did, chose to speak to Jesus and he went by night to see the Lord. Nicodemus acknowledged that Jesus was from heaven.

Jesus, then answered him and said to him "...Verily, verily, I say unto thee, Except a man be born again, he cannot see the kingdom of God" (John 3:3).

Nicodemus asked Him as to how a man can be born when he is old and wondered how he could enter second time into his mother's womb to be born again. Then Jesus said to him that unless a man is born of water and of the spirit he cannot enter into the kingdom of God. (Ref. John 3:4-5)

Saul trembled and astonished and called Jesus as "Lord". Thereafter he sought from the Lord as to what the Lord wants him to do. The Lord answered and said to him to go into the city where he will be told what he should do. Saul could not see after his encounter with the Lord.

The men who were accompanying him stood speechless when they heard voice but did not see any one there speak the words that they heard. Saul arose from the earth and could not see anybody. He was led by the men into Damascus. Paul was without sight for three days and did not eat or drink. (Ref. Acts 9:6-9)

In the meanwhile God was preparing a follower of Jesus by the name Ananias to pray over Saul. When the Lord said in a vision to Ananias to go the street called 'Straight' and inquire for Saul in the house of Judas, where Saul was praying, he was reluctant to go because he knew the trespasses that Saul did to Christians. However, when the Lord said to Ananias that Saul was a chosen vessel unto Him to bear His name before the Gentiles, the kings, and the children of Israel and that He will show how great things he should suffer for His sake Ananias went to Saul and prayed over him. Ananias called Saul as "Brother Saul" and went on saying that Lord Jesus who appeared to Saul said to him that he may receive sight and be filled with Holy Ghost. Immediately there fell from Saul's eyes scales and he received his sight and received Holy Ghost and was then baptized.

"And one Ananias, a devout man according to the law, having a good report of all the Jews which dwelt there, came unto me, and stood, and said unto me, Brother Saul, receive thy sight. And the same hour I looked up upon him". (Acts 22:12-13)

After Saul received his sight he ate food and was strengthened. He spent few days with the disciples at Damascus and preached Gospel of Grace of God in synagogues that Lord Jesus Christ was the Son of God.

Saul did missionary work of Lord Jesus Christ and he was known by the name "Paul' thereafter. Paul's title was "Apostle" i.e. A person sent out with commission to execute some business, more appropriately to preach the Gospel of Lord Jesus Christ.

Paul's missionary work was great and he was arrested twice, suffered imprisonment even though there were no legitimate charges filed against him. He was not found guilty of any charges that could lead him to be put to death.

"But none of these things move me, neither count I my life dear unto myself, so that I might finish my course with joy, and the ministry, which I have received of the Lord Jesus, to testify the gospel of the grace of God". (Acts 20:24)

Paul had great desire to go back to Jerusalem from Miletus after addressing the elders from Ephesus. When they all gathered Paul said that from the first day that he was there in Asia, he was serving the Lord with all humility of mind, and with many tears, and temptations that he faced to preach to Jews and face their wrath. He says he kept back nothing that was beneficial from anyone but preached to them publicly and from house to house testifying both to Jews and Gentiles all alike repentance toward God and faith in Lord Jesus Christ. He was not sure what problems he would encounter at Jerusalem, in future, but then, he says he does not count his life dear unto himself because he desires to finish his course with joy, and ministry that he received from the Lord Jesus Christ to testify the Gospel of grace of God. (Ref. Acts 20:19-25)

The life of Christian is to run a race to wrestle against competitors like principalities, rulers of darkness and against spiritual wickedness in high places and score victory over them.

Paul suffered for Christ's sake and established many Churches. There are 13 epistles and the book of Hebrews to his credit in the New Testament. The following references are from Paul's writings where he said that he finished his course with joy and testified the Gospel of Grace of God.

"Know ye not that they which run in a race run all, but one receiveth the prize? So run, that ye may obtain". (1 Corinthians 9:24)

When Paul was in Corinth he alluded to the games that are hosted in the Olympic stadium where running was one of the major events where many run but only one receives prize. By this statement Paul was not saying that in Christian life many run but only one or few receive salvation, but his point was that every Christian should run race with such vigor and in such a manner that he/she receives his/her crown of righteousness from the Lord at the judgment seat of Christ.

Salvation of a Christian is never lost. It is the rewards that are given at the judgment seat of Christ for the good works done by the believers that he was talking about in 1 Corinthians 9:24

"Holding forth the word of life; that I may rejoice in the day of Christ, that I have not run in vain, neither laboured in vain". (Philippians 2:16)

Every Christian is obligated to bring fruit unto the Lord. The Lord said he that does not remain in Him and does not bring fruit unto him will be cut off. This again does not mean that a person loses his/her salvation but it means that he will be cut off from bringing fruits in case he/she does not remain in Him. Jesus also said that without remaining in Him a man can do nothing.

"I am the vine, ye are the branches: He that abideth in me, and I in him, the same bringeth forth much fruit: for without me ye can do nothing". (John 15:5)

 Neither there was any god before Jesus Christ nor there any god after Him. He is Alpha and Omega.

"I am Alpha and Omega, the beginning and the end, the first and the last". (Revelation 22:13)

"Ye are my witnesses, saith the LORD, and my servant whom I have chosen: that ye may know and believe me, and understand that I am he: before me there was no God formed, neither shall there be after me". (Isaiah 43:10)

The writer of Hebrews exhorts us to lay aside every sin which does easily beset us. He instructs us to run the race with patience that is set before us.

"Wherefore seeing we also are compassed about with so great a cloud of witnesses, let us lay aside every weight, and the sin which doth so easily beset us, and let us run with patience the race that is set before us" (Hebrews 12:1)

www.ingramcontent.com/pod-product-compliance
Lightning Source LLC
Chambersburg PA
CBHW060319050426
42449CB00011B/2559